FAREWELL MILAG

by

ARTHUR H. (DICK) BIRD M.B.E.

First published in 1995
by Literatours
63 Bohemia Road, St. Leonards-on-Sea
East Sussex TN37 6RG

Copyright © British Red Cross Society 1995
Typeset & printed by The Weald Press
St. Leonards-on-Sea, East Sussex
Front cover illustration by John Plumb
5 Linton Road, Hastings, East Sussex

ISBN 0 9513475 1 9

British Library Cataloguing in Publication Data.
A catalogue record for this book is available
from the British Library.

Arthur H. (Dick) Bird, M.B.E.

PREFACE

The story told in this book had been in my mind for forty years waiting for the leisure to put it into print.

At this date, I have had two motives for undertaking the labour. The first is the ambition to make enough money out of the work to be able to donate a substantial sum (of money) to the British Red Cross Society and the Order of St. John of Jerusalem who, with the International Red Cross, enabled my camp mates and me to come through our imprisonment sound in body and mind.

The second is to pay tribute to that splendid body of men, The Merchant Navy, by recording, as well as truthfully as it lies within my powers, some impression of their steadfast courage in adversity and their achievements in creating, not only a mere modus vivende, but a mini civilization in a desert place.

It is my regret that someone better qualified than myself has not written the history of Marlag and Milag Nord, for as will become apparent in the story, I enjoyed its hospitality for less than two years.

So although I have attempted to convey in outline some historical facts for the record, my main concern has been to give impressions of my personal experience of life behind barbed-wire fences as background to the rest of my narrative.

The writing about Milag and camp life proved to be the hardest part of my undertaking. For reviving my own memory of those days far astern, I have had many conversations and correspondence with old comrades. But, as is natural, there has crept in the human tendency to forget the dreadful episodes and remember the highlights such as the arrival of parcels from the Red Cross.

Another difficulty I experienced was that of conveying adequately the sense of the initial shock of imprisonment yet elation at being alive when shipmates were dead, and to express the feelings of gloom, depression at bad news, boredom, impotence and sheer physical misery that was inevitably woven into the fabric of our lives.

A further problem has been that of deciding whose names to

mention and whose to omit. I felt, in general, constrained to name only key figures but in doing so I fear I will, through faulty memory and lack of records, have left out many whose service to their fellows deserves a place in even such a sketchy record as this work.

One supposes that the general reader would not wish the narrative to be laced with personal names, apart from the necessity of distinguishing the different characters in the story, so I hope such readers will overlook any superfluous use of names which may have crept in for sentimental reasons.

Written by A. H. Bird, 1983.

As A. H. Bird died before this book was published, his widow and sister have now carried out his wishes, and they would like to thank all those who have contributed to its production.

The proceeds from its sale will be donated to the British Red Cross Society and the Order of St. John.

Arthur Bird, was the only Merchant Navy seaman to make a successful escape from Milag Nord.

CONTENTS

Chapter		Page
1	Rude Awakening	1
2	Predator At Sea	9
3	Komet Runs The Gauntlet	22
4	Marlag And Milag Nord	31
5	Dual Control	48
6	The Third Degree	57
7	The Melting Pot	63
8	The Anatomy Of Milag	69
9	Curtain Up	82
10	Sport In Milag	94
11	Food For Thought	104
12	The Watershed	111
13	Setting Course For Freedom	121
14	Road To The Sea	133
15	The Kap Horn	145
16	Stowaway	156
17	Stockholm Interlude	164
18	Edel's Story	168
Appendix 1	German Rations	180
Appendix 2	British Red Cross Food Parcels	182
Appendix 3	Canadian Parcels	183
Appendix 4	Extracts from the Log of Cadet William Errington, ex-S.S. DEVON	184

LIST OF ILLUSTRATIONS

Illustration	Page
Arthur H. (Dick) Bird, M.B.E.	iii
M.V. AUSTRALIND	ix
The German 'raider' KOMET	8
The Milag Nord Camp	34
My Identity Card	34
Barrack 15	39
Glimpse of Hospital from Room 3, Barrack 15	40
Two views of the Milag Nord Camp	49
Plan of Milag Nord	71
Souvenir Programme	89-92
Letter concerning Bootery	116
M.S. LUOSSA	158
Dick and Edel Bird's Wedding Photograph	179

M.V. AUSTRALIND

CHAPTER ONE

Rude Awakening

M.V. AUSTRALIND of London, was gently rolling in the long, deep-blue Pacific swells in the brilliant sunshine of the tropical afternoon. She was a fine 5,000 ton merchant ship with an air of breeding about her in spite of her drab wartime paint. At this date, 14th August, 1941, she was thirteen months out of Bristol, having in the meantime shipped war materials to Egypt by the long haul round the Cape, salt from the pans near Suez to Calcutta and oriental foodstuffs from India and Burma across the world to a string of West Indian islands. Then on to the 'States' to load general cargo for Australia, and now laden, with zinc ore, honey and dried fruits, she was nearing the Galapagos Islands at her stately nine knots, heading for Panama, homeward bound.

'Homeward Bound'!! Words that stir something inside even the hardiest seaman, but this time the glow of anticipation was darkened by the threat of the U-boat packs prowling the Western Ocean, and now known to be active in the Caribbean as well. For months the war at sea had seemed blissfully remote from the crew of AUSTRALIND. Occasional reports of distant enemy activity sharpened the eyes of the look-outs watching, watching, watching. But in their minds the real menace was the U-boat a few days ahead on the other side of the Canal. The Captain obviously was taking no chances. The lifeboats' gear and provisions were being carefully overhauled. The gun's crew was well drilled, but I decided, as the Third Mate and Gunnery Officer, to give them an additional polish and spent several watches below constructing a floating target to provide realistic shooting practice.

I was rather proud of that target. It was well withstanding a rough launching. A triangle of stout planks, with an oil drum fixed under each corner for buoyancy, formed the base. On top was a pyramid of canvas painted with bright yellow and red bands that would be visible for several miles. Now complete, it sat on the after hatch.

My intention was to launch it secretly one afternoon in collusion with the Second Mate. He was to sound the Klaxon for Action Stations. We had agreed not to do it today for I needed the rest. So, after relieving the Second on the bridge for lunch, I stretched myself out on my settee. As I dozed I mused upon my fate. It was not a bad life at sea, I thought, though it was a painful wrench to be cut off from my fiancée, probably for the duration. I had been several years in a shore job, and although it was classed as a 'reserved occupation', my firm had kindly granted my wish to go back to sea. Some might think that an odd way to seek consolation, I murmured to myself as I fell asleep.

Gurr, rurr, rurr, rurr went the raucous Klaxon. In a flash I was awake and shot off the settee, reached for my tin hat and put on my lifejacket. I was shaking with rage. What a rotten joke the Second Mate was playing! After all, I was the Gunnery Officer. Bang went a gun. Damn it! He might have had the decency to let me open fire. Crash! The whole ship shook and the electric fan was wrenched off the bulkhead and flung on to the deck at me feet. My God! Someone is shooting at us! Bang – pause – crash! All Hell seemed let loose. I went out into the blinding tropical sunshine to go on the bridge for orders – no use expecting to get any sense out of the gun platform telephone. Bang! A shell smashed into the upper bridge. I saw the radio direction-finding loop aerial had been blown off and now stuck grotesquely into the fore side of the funnel. Lucky I wasn't a foot higher up the ladder at that instant, else my hand would have been blown off. Up I now went. Debris was scattered all over the lower bridge. Our young Captain Stevens lay at the fore end. I gently moved him. There was a gash in the left side of his neck. He was dead. A fine man, killed on his first command. So this is war! These were fleeting thoughts. This was time for action. I ran on to the bridge. It was so eerie. Not a soul to be seen. Neither Second Mate, Radio Officer nor Helmsman was there. All gone within the odd minute, blown overboard perhaps.

With sense heightened by the emergency, I took the situation in at a glance. Wheelhouse and radio room a shambles. Steering gear and engine-room telegraph wrecked. The ship was going round in circles out of control.

In the offing, right in the glare of the sun, was the cause of the trouble. A smallish merchant ship with side plates strangely hinged up exposing a broadside of big guns trained on AUSTRALIND. A big Nazi war flag flying from her main gaff did away with the necessity of further introduction. Making straight for the Chartroom, I quickly searched in the wreckage and found the weighted canvas bag containing the code book and other secret papers, all done up ready for such a moment as this. I dumped it into the sea from the starboard wing of the bridge, out of sight of the enemy. Nothing more could be done on the bridge. How the devil could we stop the engine? I turned to go down. The German had stopped shelling. The boat deck was afire. The lifeboats were splintered and one of the falls had been cut. To try to fire the 4.7 inch gun on the stern would be a useless gesture and probably suicidal.

I went down on the main deck where it was a relief to see living men again. Most of the crew were mustering amidships and the First Mate, Ronald Willoughby, had assumed command. After the first rude shock and the reactions prompted by instinct or duty, the extent of the damage began to be taken in and the general situation appreciated. 'Sparks', Chief Radio Officer Hearden, who had been shot in the arm while gallantly persisting in sending the QQQQ[1] message, was sitting on the deck where the Chief Steward, Harry Gray, had propped him up against the bulkhead as comfortably as possible. A shell had gone through the engineers' accommodation, killing young Douglas Beardsall, the Fourth Engineer, wrapping a steel plate round him as he lay in his bunk. Tommy Curran, the Fifth Engineer, a jovial Irishman, was seriously wounded and was being carried on deck. The Second Mate, J. Y. Morgan, was there; he was wounded in the thigh. How he and the helmsman had got off the bridge without running into me was a mystery. AUSTRALIND was losing way because Harry Gray, a man of great common sense and courage, correctly assuming the telegraph and steering gear were broken, had rushed to the engine room and told Jim Daly, the Third Engineer, who was on watch, to stop the engine.

---

[1] *QQQQ signified an armed merchant ship;
RRRR a warship; SSSS a submarine.*

Men from the crew's quarters aft said the Germans had shot at the 4.7 inch gun and one shell had struck the deck and ricocheted off without exploding. It was not known whether the hull had been holed so, as zinc concentrates are not much more buoyant than lead, a quick decision was made to launch the two jolly boats which seemed to have escaped damage. Thoughts by some of sneaking away in the starboard boat, which was out of sight of the Germans, were reluctantly abandoned. 'Sparks' doubted if his signal had got out unjammed. Although barely 300 miles from the Galapagos Islands, the noon sights had confirmed that the South Equatorial Current was running at 1½ knots away from the islands and the wind was unfavourable as well. The chance of making the Marquesas Islands, some 2,000 miles away, seemed remote, even if the Germans connived at the escape.

By this time the enemy ship had come closer and had launched a large motor boat which, with spray flying from her bows, was fast approaching the stricken AUSTRALIND. As we were putting Mr. Curran in the port-side jolly boat, the launch came alongside. It was full of husky sun-burnt men, stripped to the waist and heavily armed; and there were things in the bottom of the boat that looked like explosive devices. An officer dressed in the tropical uniform of the Kriegsmarine climbed the pilot ladder put over the jolly boat. As he swung jauntily over the rail, he said, 'Gentlemen, for you the war is over, you have twenty minutes to pack a few personal things and put them in your boat. We will take your wounded to our ship first and will take you later.'

The pirates climbed on board and proceeded to ransack the ship. AUSTRALIND's crew went to their quarters (those that had not been destroyed by shell fire) to select essential items of clothing, and between them assembled the strange assortment of objects that men under great stress and excitement seem prone to grasp at.

The Germans had taken poor Tommy Curran from the jolly boat to the raider's sick bay and now ordered the crew to leave the ship. Seabags and suitcases were stowed in the jolly boat and all hands were ordered to board the motor launch. The First Mate considered it a point of honour to be the last to leave.

It was a strange and depressing experience to abandon dear old

AUSTRALIND and dead shipmates there on the vast lonely ocean, that fine ship, from Denny's famous yard at Dumbarton on the Clyde, which had been our home for so long, and those men with whom we had shared the vicissitudes of life at sea. As the launch went bounding over the Pacific swells, with the jolly boat's painter jerking taut then splashing slack in the sea, we took our last look at her. She was wallowing in the troughs, battered and forlorn, afire midships, lifeboat davits swinging aimlessly as she rolled; and to give an eerie touch to the dismal scene a large black frigate bird circled above her.

There was also time to look at the German. She was supposed to be a neutral Japanese cargo ship (the Pearl Harbour calamity had not yet occurred). There was her name RYOKO MARU painted on her bows and a prominent Japanese flag on her side which at the moment had a swastika draped over it. Seamen's eyes took in the details. A smallish ship, more likely to have been built for the Mediterranean trade than for long ocean voyages. The side plating had been hinged down again, so the main armament could not be seen. The big stern-chaser was still exposed and it looked to be of at least 6-inch calibre. There were smaller bore weapons mounted at many vantage points.

An accommodation ladder was lowered and we scrambled aboard. We were mustered on the main deck, searched, counted and herded for'rd on to a small well-deck, then through a steel-barred door in the fo'c's'le bulkhead and down below. The door slammed to behind us with an ominous 'clank' followed by the loud 'clonk' of a key in the lock. The door led down to a companionway into the top deck of No. 1 hold. Part of the space, we noticed, had been converted into WCs and crude washing facilities. There was also a smallish room with bunks into which the not-too-seriously wounded Second Mate and Chief Radio Officer were put. The ratings and cadets were ordered to occupy the rest of the deck. Down another narrow companionway we arrived at the officers' 'guest room'. This was on the waterline and there were no portholes to give natural light or ventilation. Dismountable tables and forms ran fore and aft near the ship's side. There were steel lockers on the forward bulkhead. Everything was starkly utilitarian but clean and shipshape.

Eventually, we received from the Germans, clothing, toiletries and other articles we had been allowed to salvage from our ship. Cameras and sextants were among the things withheld. There was some sharing of gear with shipmates whose accommodation had been wrecked in the action. But in the prevailing tropical weather few garments were needed. I found sharing my toothbrush something of a novelty. And so we began to shake down.

The man least pleased with our new status was our Bosun, A. Jesson, of Chatham. As a young man, he had been captured by the German warship MOWE in the Great War.

After what seemed many hours, the seamen chosen to be 'peggies'[1] were ordered to go to the galley under armed guard, to collect our first meal. When the bulk ration was brought back it was divided into equal portions by Mr. Willoughby, our Chief Officer. This became a routine which was carried out with meticulous fairness under the sharp eyes of our hungry crew throughout the voyage. Each man had been issued with a gaudy, enamelled plate, a brown, enamelled mug and a spoon, and now received his diminutive piece of canned meat, a slice of 'black' bread and marge. At the same time we were introduced to the staple beverage of the Third Reich, *ersatz* coffee.

At the end of this feverish day each man was issued with two dark-brown blankets, which were clean and dry. Then we had to learn how to rig the hammocks provided. They were not of the swinging variety used in those days in His Majesty's warships. Merchant seamen, incidentally, always slept in rigid bunks. The basic parts were rectangles of stout canvas which formed the actual hammocks and pairs of wire ropes, the ends of which had to be made fast and taut between the deck and deckhead (ceiling). There was one set of wires at the head and another at the foot of each hammock position, and the corners of the canvases had to be attached to them, in pairs, one above the other. Wooden stretchers placed between the wires prevented the sides of the hammocks coming together when

---

[1]*In the days when a member of the crew had to fetch the food for the watch from the galley, in tinned pans called 'kits', to eat in the fo'c's'le, that man, or boy, was known as the 'peggy'. The term was, of course, used by us on the raider and subsequently.*

occupied. When we had got the hang of it and rows of hammocks were set up, we turned in on our first night as prisoners – each man reliving the violent excitement and turbulent emotions of this fateful afternoon, until falling asleep from sheer exhaustion.

The German 'raider' KOMET

CHAPTER TWO

Predator At Sea

Early next morning we were awakened by brisk martial music from the loudspeaker installed in the room. And so began the basic routine of our life on the pirate ship; unship and stow the hammocks; ablutions; 'Peggies' to the galley for the rations (always under guard and no officers allowed to go); rig up the tables and forms; breakfast of rye bread with a smear of marge and a red nondescript jam washed down with *ersatz* coffee; clean out quarters.

Soon we heard that our jovial shipmate, Tommy Curran, had died in the sick bay during the night and that his body had been committed to the deep. Though not unexpected in view of his condition after the action, the news was depressing and was a foretaste of many a dose of gloom that inevitably weighs heavy on the spirits of helpless captives.

The German officer in charge of prisoners also informed us that we could take exercise on the well-deck and the fo'c's'le head. Slightly to our surprise, it became apparent that we would be permitted to walk or sit up there for the greater part of each day. Armed guards were always stationed at the heads of the two ladders leading from our well-deck, ready to stop anyone attempting to go aft. Apart from their presence, there were no unreasonable restrictions on our movements. Of course, with No. 1 hatch coaming taking up most of the small well-deck and the usual windlass, bitts and ventilators cluttering the fo'c's'le head, there wasn't much room: in fact, nineteen paces were the most one could take in a straight line – provided no-one else was in the way.

Nevertheless, it was good to be able to scan the horizon and to watch the flying fish, startled by the on-coming bows, perform their remarkable feats of gliding over the bright blue waves. There was also much interest aboard the raider to attract and hold the attention. The very idea of being aboard a German ship with German seamen all about us – real, tangible Germans, the enemy – yet all of us in the same little ship, seemed fantastic. Who could fail to be astonished to see a lookout in a swivelling chair at the very top of the tall foremast with very large and doubtless, powerful, binoculars mounted on the truck? In the prevailing clear weather they would have seen some 20ft of AUSTRALIND's masts before our lookout in the crow's nest, hardly above the crosstrees, could possibly have seen a yard of their topmast peeping over the horizon some fifteen miles away. It made one realize how vulnerable a merchant ship was to detection and ultimate capture.

It was noticeable that the raider did not move much. Sometimes one felt the engine driving her ahead slowly, often she would be stationery for hours on end, lolling about in the gentle swell. She worked her way up to the Galapagos Islands, for we saw land in the distance within a couple of days of our capture.

As we were entering on our third day of captivity and beginning to get used to the simple routine of prison life, the alarm broke the silence of that Sunday morning. We were sunning ourselves on deck and were immediately hustled below. The engine started, the ship throbbed into life and we heard the bow-wave hissing past the ship's side. Various other whirring and clanking noises were heard that we didn't comprehend. We sat on our benches, tense and expectant. At about 10.45 am a loud report indicated that the raider had fired one of her guns. Soon a broadside was fired. Our hearts sank within us as we imagined what was going on. The gunfire did not last long, and the raider eventually stopped. We had what seemed a long wait before we knew what had happened. Then our lives took on a new dimension with the arrival of the Captain and some Officers of the Dutch cargo ship KOTA NOPAN, who told their story. When the neutral 'Japanese' had been sighted, they turned away from her and headed at full speed for the shelter of the Galapagos Islands some forty miles away. When the German war flag was hoisted and a warning shot fired, they tried to get out the QQQQ signal by radio and bravely fired a couple of 4-inch shells at the raider. These activities provoked the Germans to open fire in earnest. As things hotted up, KOTA NOPAN was stopped and her boats lowered, then the shelling ceased. It was a relief to our pent up emotions to hear that no lives were lost. Apparently the Germans knew of the valuable cargo aboard her and wished to preserve the ship.

We 'old lags' did our best to make the new arrivals welcome in 'our' end of the ship. In their turn, Captain Hatenboer, Chief Officer Strickers, Second Officer Pete Bos, Junior Officer Tuinhout and Chief Radio Officer Paalingdood in due course enriched our existence by their personalities and by their material help. Like all Dutch mariners, they spoke perfect English. Their fellow officers and the Japanese crew were left aboard their ship with a German prize crew in control.

Next morning, when we were allowed on deck, we could see KOTA NOPAN for ourselves. She lay a short distance away, stopped like the raider, rolling gently in the swell. There was great activity on both ships and boats bustled to and fro between them, for the Germans were busy transferring some of KOTA NOPAN's cargo of tin ingots. This looked like piracy indeed, and the appearance of the husky, sunburnt seamen stripped to the waist manning the boats in the plundering operations heightened the impression the scene made upon us. Although it was a melancholy sight for our Dutch friends, it held us all spellbound.

All through the next day the work continued until late afternoon when there was great commotion. 'Action Stations' sounded. A ship had been sighted. Boats were recalled, prisoners were bundled down below, and soon the raider was quivering under full power ahead. Again we sat below helpless, our stomachs turning over at the sounds we could now identify and the scene we could imagine. We heard the rattle of the ammunition hoist in its trunking running through our accommodation, and recognized the heavy steely 'clonk' when the side plating was hinged up to expose the guns. The suspense culminated in the crash of gunfire. What poor devils were being shot to bits now? The thought was going through every prisoner's mind. The raider stopped and rolled in the gentle swell. We waited. Eventually our door clanked open and men's feet clumped down the companionways. Britishers! Captain Redwood, flushed in the face and parched of throat by his shocking ordeal, asked for a drink of water and I gave it to him out of my brown enamelled mug. The story was soon tumbling out in the manner of men who have just undergone a shocking experience and are glad to find themselves still alive. DEVON, a British India Steam Navigation Co.'s ship, was the victim. There had been no resistance, so she was spared a pounding and none of her crew of 144 was injured. Of the total complement 113 were Indians and they were transferred to the holds of KOTA NOPAN. The 31 Britishers who were the deck Officers, Engineers, Radio Officers and Chief Steward were put aboard the raider. DEVON was scuttled.

The newcomers had sailed from a British port barely a month before, so we of AUSTRALIND, who had been away from home over a year, and had left before the 'blitz', were hungry for uncensored news of how things really were in Britain. Their reports of the devastation did not impress us unduly, for that aspect had been broadcast worldwide; we knew about it and had adjusted to the situation. We wanted to know what life was like and what was the spirit of the people. Their answers were a tonic for our morale.

After this third capture near the Galapagos Islands, KOMET – for that we learnt was the German ship's real name – began to work her way very slowly south-west along the Australasia-Panama shipping route. Sometimes under way at low speed, sometimes stopped, but always watching, watching, and KOTA NOPAN accompanied her. Tropical day followed glorious tropical day and we captives began to get into the new very simple lifestyle. We also began to glean little bits of information about our captors. With our formerly acquired knowledge of our enemy in the back of our minds, we noticed no-one gave the Nazi salute nor was a 'Heil Hitler' ever heard. The Commander invited the prisoner-Captains to have a drink with him on Sunday mornings and it was one of their observations that only a photograph of Admiral Raeder was hanging in the wardroom; Hitler's was never seen.

Somehow we discovered that the Commander had the rank of Rear Admiral and that his name was Eyssen. When on his rounds he came to the break of the well-deck and looked down on us, we eyed him with critical curiosity. He was a shortish, stockily built man, square headed but not particularly teutonic in general appearance. His features indicated a very firm but not unkindly character and reminded one slightly of Admiral Beatty, particularly because he wore his cap at a somewhat rakish angle. Though he was the author of our predicament and master of our fate, I for one, oddly enough, did not feel much animosity towards him. Nor could one hate his second-in-command who had served as a Mate in the British Elder Dempster Line between the wars. He, it was, who sent down a ration of cigarettes soon after our capture and they were a great boon to the smokers. The Bosun too, though he had no dealings with us, was obviously a seaman and leader of character. We could see the officers on the bridge and ratings about the deck keeping watch, taking sights and going about their normal duties, just as we had done until a few days before. Perhaps it was not too fanciful to think that after all there really was a brotherhood of the sea. At least we perceived that there was no threat of ill-treatment.

Of course, we had no inkling of KOMET's activities before our capture. The only trace of previous occupation by prisoners was the name Felix Fagan scratched on the back of one of the gaudily decorated Japanese enamelled plates issued to us. One of our number said he had been a shipmate of Fagan, but that tenuous connection gave us no clue as to what ship he was on when captured, nor of the date of his confinement on the raider. It did, however, seem to indicate that prisoners were not left aboard indefinitely; and there was food for speculation in that thought.

There were no reliable signs as to how long KOMET had been at sea. One of our hammocks bore the black, stencilled marks DANZIG 1940, but who could say what that meant in this connection. We had reason to suspect she had been out a good while because of an unusual activity that excited our curiosity just now. The crew had a heavy contraption on deck consisting essentially of pieces of planks hinged together to form a flexible 'mat'. Each piece of timber had large stout wire broom heads fixed on it, the bristles all facing the same way. Its purpose was soon demonstrated. By means of wire ropes passed under the hull, and worked by winches, the gigantic scrubbing brush was dragged to and fro across the ship's bottom to remove barnacles and any other marine growth that would reduce the ship's speed. How effective it was we had no means of discovering and, though we felt our best interests would be served by the shaggiest possible speed damper that old Neptune could provide, it was a novel and fascinating exercise to watch.

The days rolled slowly by and built up into weeks, with only one alarm for 'Action Stations'. Smoke had been seen on the horizon late one afternoon and, with all the normal rush and clamour, KOMET set off in pursuit. Much to our satisfaction, no action ensued. Whether the ship out-distanced 'us' or was neutral we never discovered.

In this period the genius of merchant seamen for amusing themselves, even in adverse circumstances, began to emerge. AUSTRALIND's Chippy, Michael Marks, organized a simple concert party which put on a couple of shows including high-kicking chorus girls. I was one of the latter and Micky taught us the steps in the washroom. It didn't seem to matter that I wore a beard!

The Germans provided us with a few books written in English. One that came into my hands was 'Predictions for the year 1939' by the then famous seer 'Petulengro'. Chapter one began, 'There will be no war in 1939.' I read no more of it. A copy of the *Sydney Bulletin*, which doubtless had been in the mailbag carried by AUSTRALIND, contained an article of more immediate interest to us. Entitled 'Life on a German Raider', it was written by one of a lucky group of prisoners who were put ashore and left on a Pacific island. This was heartening news and planted in us the hope that we might be disposed of in a similar fashion.

The Dutchmen had been permitted to bring a number of books from KOTA NOPAN, including Pear's Encyclopedia which contained a small atlas. Although we were just about as far from Germany as it is possible to be, the dreadful thought that our captors might try to get us there lurked in the back of our minds. This led me to take a keen interest in the little map of Germany and to memorize the relative positions of the principal cities. I discovered a simple way of doing so. If one takes the city of Hanover as the centre of a compass, then Hamburg is practically due north. Then, 'boxing the compass', one finds a principal city on twenty-one of the thirty-two points of the compass. It was only a matter of learning and remembering which city corresponded to which compass point.

The Dutchmen also introduced us to the Chinese game of Mah-Jong. They had brought a set with them, with German approval, and this enabled the non-card players to while away pleasantly many otherwise monotonous hours.

After a month of uneventful meandering in the vast Pacific, sighting nothing except the distant silhouette of an island which the watchmen recognized as one of the Tuamota group, the even tenor of our existence was broken in an unexpected fashion on 20th September, 1941. The alarm sounded for Action Stations, and once again our bowels seemed to knot up inside us. Hustled down below, we could only listen to the noises and use our imagination. However, not shot was heard. The ship stopped. What had happened? We had the answer when we were next permitted on deck. KOMET had rendezvoused with another raider, ATLANTIS. Soon a lively traffic in motor launches was under way among the three ships, KOTA NOPAN having resumed her station with KOMET after precautionary identification of ATLANTIS. This was indeed a sight for ocean-bored eyes. A fine big merchant ship, perhaps a third larger than her little sister, double her tonnage and doubtless much faster. Her tall foremast carried a look-out man with large binoculars at the truck, a good 100ft above the waterline, and at the highly placed crosstrees, perhaps only 25ft lower, two more men in separate crow's-nests supplemented the vigilant eyes aloft on KOMET. The most exciting thing about this rendezvous for us prisoners was the transfer of other luckless mariners from ATLANTIS: men from TOTTENHAM and BALZAC, all with their own stories of peril, terror and bravery, and an unusual civilian from ZAM ZAM. Their arrival in our midst naturally caused something of an upheaval in the snug little lifestyle we had created in our cramped quarters during the last listless weeks. What an amazing capacity we humans have for 'settling in'!

There was more excitement the next day when a supply ship, MUNSTERLAND, arrived from Japan to join the party. We were fascinated by the sight of oil pipes being rigged between the two sizeable ships rolling close together in the swell and had to admire the skilful seamanship of the operation. There was a constant shuttling of boats laden with stores and equipment for both raiders, and the further transfer and share-out of KOTA NOPAN's tin, to increase the chance of some of it reaching Germany, we supposed. The raiders' crews were also actively engaged in ship visiting and we caught sight of Captain Rogge, commander of ATLANTIS, when Admiral Eyssen showed him around KOMET. For all their brave show we sensed our captors were constantly aware of the risk of an encounter with something that could hit back, and that they were lonely men far from home in time and distance. The meeting with their compatriots must have eased tensions for the moment, but soon they would be slipping back alone into the solitude and peril of the great oceans.

During this fascinating gathering of enemy ships young Neil Brodie, one of the cadets off DEVON, decided without reference to anyone else to make sketches of ATLANTIS and the supply ship, in case an opportunity ever presented itself to pass them on to the Royal Navy. He worked in the shelter of No. 1 hatch. I was surprised to see what he was up to and appalled to notice that a guard on the deck above had spotted him. I nipped over to him, out of sight of the guard, and told him to get rid of the drawings as soon as possible. He went below in haste and flushed them down a WC. He immediately returned on deck, and by the time an officer arrived to investigate, he was quietly sketching prisoners sprawling around the hatch. The German was foiled but not completely convinced of his innocence. Neil was lucky to get off with a warning and the relatively light penalty of washing down the alleyways and cleaning the WCs in the prisoners' quarters for the rest of the voyage.

After the three-day rendezvous, KOMET changed course. Whereas she had worked roughly south-west from the Galapagos to the meeting place, which we estimated to be about half-way between Panama and New Zealand, she now headed south-east. This provoked much speculation as to our destination. Obviously we would fetch up at Cape Horn if we maintained this course. What then? The shipping lanes off the South African coast? The Indian Ocean, or Europe?

From our new shipmates we gleaned some information about ATLANTIS and her crew, and especially concerning an enigmatic character, one Frank Vicovari, still aboard her in the sick-bay. He had been badly injured at the capture of ZAM ZAM, five months before, and was still too incapacitated to be transferred to KOMET. His story struck the imagination for several reasons. ZAM ZAM we knew as an Egyptian ship and therefore technically a neutral, for AUSTRALIND had been docked near her in Alexandria. It was an irony of fate that in the dawning ATLANTIS had mistaken her for one of the British Bibby Liners which the Germans knew were being used as troopers. She had indeed belonged to that fleet, all of which were unmistakably characterized by four tall masts. Her name had been LEICESTERSHIRE before sale to Société Misr de Navigation Maritime of Egypt. The irony was compounded by the fact that Mr. Vicovari was a citizen of the United States of America (as were 137 more of the 202 passengers ultimately landed safely in France by a German supply ship and repatriated) which was not at war with the Axis powers at that date. What especially endeared us to him were stories of his implacable hostility to his captors. Though physically helpless and isolated in a sick-bay he would needle them at every opportunity.

A British civilian passenger, Albert A. Starling, had lain in the sick-bay with Vicovari for a while. His arrival on KOMET projected a markedly different personality and background into our nautical community. He was middle-aged and had recently completed a course in chiropractic in the USA. He had been on his way to South Africa to take up practice there. Chiropractic was something quite new to us, but we were soon to hear all about it. We were told that if one were to be, and remain, healthy it was essential to have all one's vertebrae 'in adjustment', that is to say, perfectly lined up so that none put pressure on the spinal chord and caused pain or malfunction in some part of the body. The role of the chiropractor, it seemed was to detect misalignments and bring about their 'adjustment'. Then the natural defence-mechanisms within a man's body could cope with and overcome illness. Sore throats, headaches, digestive disorders and so on, were supposed to respond to this treatment. To laymen this line of argument, expounded with gravity and sincerity, was quite persuasive. Someone recalled a shipmate whose vision was impaired after a spinal injury. It tied up, didn't it? But when Mr. Starling continued with the story of a man – was he the Principal of the U.S. college where he got his training? – who ate typhus germs on toast to provide the immunity of a properly adjusted body, eyebrows were politely raised. Despite his whiff of quackery, some with minor ailments were ready to undergo treatment and I for one enjoyed the diversion which these demonstrations of the art provided. After a tactile examination of the neck region, the 'patient', if deemed to be 'out of adjustment', would be laid down on his side on a table, his head supported by a firm pillow formed by a tightly rolled jacket. The chiropractor would take up a suitable position to place the side of his left hand on the patient's neck at the appropriate vertebrae and apply some pressure, then with his right hand upon the left give it a sudden jerk. Our Chief Steward, a real countryman at heart, who underwent treatment and thought he benefited from it, always referred to the final action as 'the rabbit punch'. Whether one accepted the explanation of chiropractic or remained sceptical of it, one could not fail to be diverted by Mr. Starling's demonstrations.

From TOTTENHAM's survivors we got an inkling of the horror of a sudden attack in the night without warning; and with them we pondered the fate of the seventeen of their shipmates who were believed to have evaded the Germans and got away in a lifeboat. That action had taken place 1,100 miles from Brazil, the nearest land to leeward.

Another of the newcomers from ATLANTIS began to affect our lives in a different way. He was Alf Holmes, an Engineer of TOTTENHAM and a member of the Salvation Army. We were not accustomed to men talking openly about their religious beliefs till he joined us, so felt rather shy at first. Captain Hatenboer, we already learnt from his officers, was a devout Christian; in fact, he was about to conduct the normal weekly service on KOTA NOPAN when KOMET rudely intervened. Soon after Alf arrived, they teamed up to provide the opportunity for anyone to take part in a simple act of reverence on Sunday mornings. Even to some doubters of orthodoxy, like myself, these times of reflection on the eternal verities had the salutary effect of steering our thoughts away from the perennial topics of food, cigarettes and rumours.

KOMET, still disguised as the Japanese RYOKO MARU and with KOTA NOPAN far out on the beam to widen the search area, continued to cruise at a moderate speed, generally in a south-easterly direction. No ship was chased, so presumably nothing was seen. The super-optimists persuaded themselves that we couldn't be far from Easter Island and that that was the ideal place to dump a crowd of unwanted merchant seamen. It was remote enough to enable the raider to get well away before we could raise the alarm and start a hunt, wasn't it? It all made sense, didn't it? but no island was seen, the south-easterly course was held and the weather got cooler. The role of the castaways became less attractive.

By this time Siebren Tuinhout, the Junior Officer of KOTA NOPAN, and I had started to do a bit of navigation on our own account. We had noticed that the raider kept 'zone time', so the alteration of the clocks told us when we had crossed from one zone to another and hence gave us longitude. The Dutch Second Mate, Pete Bos, had been allowed to keep a Nautical Almanac, but sextants had been taken away from them. Anyway, a sextant could not be used under the constant eyes of the guards.

Day after day we ploughed on in company with KOTA NOPAN. It became colder and spells on deck were limited to 'getting a breath of fresh air' or momentarily escaping the oppression of our crowded quarters. Many who had been captured in the tropics were beginning to feel the lack of warm clothing. Happily, our good natured Dutchmen who had been permitted to bring all their gear with them, generously made good some of the more acute deficiencies.

The South-East Traders we headed into at first slackened and then became variable. Eventually the wind veered westerly. The fleecy clouds were displaced by an unbroken layer of greyness and the seas came up big on the starboard quarter. Before long the 'Brave west wind of the Roaring Forties' was astern and drove the little ship along before mounting seas. The German crew were preparing for bad weather, lashing and securing anything that could possibly come adrift. It seemed to be getting harder to handle the ship and keep her from broaching to, and this was evidently a fear shared by the German officers, for they had a yard (doubtless one of the spare derrick booms they carried to enable them to alter the ship's appearance) rigged up on the foremast and set a large square sail on it. This had the desired effect. In the gathering gloom and mist we lost sight of KOTA NOPAN.

It was on 10th October, my birthday, that we came abeam of Cape Horn. Round the Horn, before the mast, under sail in a pirate ship! I stood on the fo'c's'le head in the gloaming of that day, holding on tightly to the handrail, the bows heaving up and rapidly dropping down into the deep troughs as the gigantic grey seas came creaming up, storm driven, from astern. The wind screamed in the rigging and I got wet. When one is inured to the hardships and fears of such a situation one can with awe and reverence appreciate the majesty of the raging elements. The consciousness of being in the uttermost part of the earth heightened the dramatic effect. As I turned to go, I looked aft and saw the head of the German officer on the bridge peering over the dodger and I wryly said to myself, as I went below, 'She's all yours now Mr. Mate, you are welcome to look after her yourself this dirty night.'

In the following days of thick, stormy weather, we had no means of telling how the ship was heading save by the direction of the wind, which had shifted from astern round to the port quarter. It looked as if we would pass between the Falkland Islands and South Georgia. KOTA NOPAN kept in contact and we often saw her surging along in the quartering seas, great black seas with foaming white crests. Occasionally a solitary albatross would be seen gliding on powerful wings along the crests of those mighty waves, effortless and serene, circling first one ship then the other: a magnificent sight.

In a spell of thick fog, somewhere between the islands, the two ships became separated and did not meet again for several days. In the meantime, in clearing weather, it was apparent that we were holding a north-easterly course, and it became warmer.

It is irksome for a navigator to be ignorant of his position and feel impotent to do anything about it. I suppose it was this sense of outraged professionalism that drove me to make a rudimentary quadrant of cardboard with a view to determining the latitude. Pete Bos had a protractor amongst his gear and it was an easy matter to divide the arc into a scale of degrees. There was a small plumbob by means of which one aligned the 90° line with the vertical. A pin was positioned so as to cast its shadow in the sunlight on to the degrees scale and so give a direct reading of the sun's altitude. When the ship was steady and the sunlight strong, it proved possible to get a 'sight' which appeared to be accurate to within a degree or two. Tuinhout was my accomplice in this activity and we found we could operate without arousing suspicion of the guards simply by having a couple of biggish fellows suitably placed to screen us from the Germans. By noting the sun's altitude when the ship's navigators were taking their noon 'sights', getting the sun's declination from Bos's almanac, one could calculate the latitude in the usual way. As mentioned, we had a fair idea of the longitude by noting when the ship's clocks were altered on entering a new time zone. Crude as our instrument was, we got to know roughly where we were on the little world map in Pear's Encyclopedia, and which way we were going.

KOMET rendezvoused KOTA NOPAN in the latitude of the River Plate far out in the ocean. On 17th October, 1941, they parted company for good. KOMET then gently cruised around 30°S and 30°W, waiting for orders it was rumoured; certainly waiting.

CHAPTER THREE

KOMET Runs The Gauntlet

When KOMET did set off it was in a south-easterly direction and this course surprised us. Furthermore, she held that course for several days. By 24th October I had become confident enough of my navigation to say, 'If we keep on this course we shall sight Tristan da Cunha tomorrow.'

When we were let up on deck next morning there it was, a blue-black mountainous mass on the horizon, our first sight of land for fifty days. Speculation about our being landed was on everyone's lips and wishful thinking produced all the reasons why we should be dumped there. After skirting the southern side of the island at a good distance, KOMET was brought round to the north-western end and taken within ten miles of the shore, where there appeared to be a good expanse of flatter land in front of the mountains. This must be the landing place! Packing our scanty possessions would not take long; and very few of us did not prepare for the expected summons to go. It was a beautifully clear, sunny afternoon. KOMET lay stationary, hour after hour. There was but a gentle breeze and consequently only a little sea running. What could the lookouts see that we couldn't? Why the delay? We could not see a sign of habitation, nor any ship or boat, let alone movement of human beings. Teatime came and went and still we remained in the same place. Obviously, it was reasoned, the Germans were waiting for the evening so they could dump us ashore and then scuttle off into the night. So, it was with a strange mixture of emotions that we looked at the inviting shore as the guards shepherded us down below at the end of the day.

Later the main engine started. This is it. She's going closer in. It was good to hear the steady beat of her motor. She's going faster! Must be full ahead now. We could hear the swish of the bow waves through the hull plating. It's an hour now since she started; she must be getting near. Stolid men tingled with excitement at the thought of stepping ashore to freedom. But KOMET's engine kept going, and going. Even so, the super-optimists thought the landing would be made the next day. At 'wakey, wakey' we noticed that the ship had stopped, and when we were let up on deck into the pleasant sunny daylight, there was not a thing in sight! For her own inscrutable reasons KOMET lay there motionless all that Sunday.

What would be the next move? Northward up the Atlantic or eastward to the Cape and beyond? Since our hopes of being landed had been completely quenched, neither alternative gave us any cheer. Northward we thought must mean Germany, a chilling thought, even though Europe was 6,000 miles away. The Cape and beyond? Was KOMET to become a latter-day 'Flying Dutchman' condemned to roam the Southern Ocean till the end of time? We were not long in suspense. The sun was ahead at noon! Of course, the Germans never deliberately told us anything about their actions or intentions, but we prisoners, seafarers ourselves, soon sensed the homeward-bound spirit in the raider's crew. She forged ahead purposefully at 10 or 12 knots in a north-north-westerly direction without any of those tedious hours, even days, of waiting for a victim to heave into sight. Before we were once more enjoying flying-fish weather, we had begun to speculate on what sort of 'homecoming' awaited us.

We were not the only persons aboard who were becoming apprehensive as to what might happen to us as we left the isolation and comparative security of the remote south. Admiral Eyssen, himself, ironically enough, turned to his captives for a morsel of comfort. A proposition was put to us that we should make a written statement to the effect that we had received humane treatment during our imprisonment on KOMET. This request provoked a lively debate. The outcome was a general agreement that, because we had been decently treated in all respects, except food, there was no element of disloyalty in stating the truth. No-one had seen, or been subjected to, any form of Nazi arrogance or rough treatment whilst on the raider, or the story would have been different. As it was, there might even be some benefit to us in meeting the German request. So we decided to give this 'life assurance' to our captors. I drafted and actually wrote the final agreed version of it.

When up in the Horse Latitudes of the North Atlantic we were treated to an unusual experience. RYOKO MARU of the Nipon Yusen Kaisha was transformed into the Portuguese SAO THOME II. She still had a white painted superstructure but the funnel was all black and, of course, the large Japanese flag on each side had to be replaced by the Portuguese colours. More fundamental were the removal of the bulwark extensions and the dummy No. 1 hatch, thus making her look what she was, in fact, a well-deck vessel. The number and disposition of the samson posts and derricks were also changed. This metamorphosis was naturally a matter of interest and even amusement to us in our tightly circumscribed little world.

What we saw when we came on deck on November 17th, about the latitude of the Azores, was a sight more sinister and one which immediately aroused mixed emotions in a British Merchant seaman. We had an escort of two submarines! One close on each side, with their markings U-516 and U-652 plainly painted on the conning towers. So these were the dreaded U-boats, the vicious enemy that attacked ships by day or night without warning; the cowardly and unchivalrous face of the Kriegsmarine. Yet now they were protecting KOMET and ourselves. There was a certain fascination in watching them.

Soon after this rendezvous, all prisoners had to watch the screening of a film, which we supposed had been brought by submarine. Our captors seemed to be embarrassed by the event, and well they might, for it was the one and only attempt at intimidating us in the whole three and a half months we were in their charge and we suspected it was none of Eyssen's doing. The movie was the German version of the evacuation of Dunkirk. It showed bedraggled columns of defeated Tommies being strafed by screeching Stukas, and all the disarray of the remnants of the British Army trying to escape in a few little boats from the invincible Wermacht. To their everlasting credit, our boys treated this with contempt, and had the author of this crude episode but known our hearts, he would have realized that the propaganda had completely backfired.

After monotonously ploughing into cold grey seas under leaden skies for six days, Sunday, 23rd November, was a day of surprises and excitement. 'Land on the starboard beam,' was the excited report of the peggies returning with our breakfast coffee. When allowed on deck, we identified it as the coast of north-west Spain.

There was another surprise; we saw that KOMET was reverting to her true colours, war-time grey. It looked as if all hands were on the job. It was not what was done so much as the speed at which it was carried out that evoked the envy of every Mate and Bosun among us. The whole ship was painted round in half a day!

The weather cleared as we neared the land, and at one stage we were sailing parallel with the coast, so close that we could see houses and trees distinctly. One was tempted to think we were inside the three-mile limit. Spain, neutral Spain, just over there!

The Royal Navy had not stopped the raider and rescued us as our feverish wishful thinking, fired perhaps by memories of the gallant ALTMARK affair, had persuaded us they would. Now we were on the doorstep of the Third Reich. This was our last chance and a number of us younger and more vigorous men seriously discussed plunging overboard and swimming ashore. The sea was moderate. It is hard to say why no-one tried it. Of course, the hazards of being picked up by the escort were considered but, in the grip of the urge to escape, we gave no thought to our physical weakness from reduced diet and lack of real training. Mercifully, a subconscious common sense prevailed and the land gradually receded.

Ever since it had become certain that KOMET was destined for Europe there had been constant speculation as to where she would attempt to dock. Until the submarine picked her up somewhere west of the Azores and she began heading eastward, it seemed possible that she might try, in the Arctic night, to make the great north-about sweep through the Denmark Strait, round to the shelter of the Norwegian coast and so to Germany. Now, the argument ran, we were heading for Bordeaux. Somebody knew someone who had been told of merchant-seamen prisoners being landed there. Well, it certainly looked like it. What could we expect? There was talk of a prison camp surrounded with barbed wire, a horrible prospect, vague though it was. After 101 days on the raider and now used to her conditions, we thought KOMET a much more desirable place of detention, even here in the Bay in winter. We would know tomorrow. This might be our last night aboard KOMET.

Next day, misty, grey and cheerless, saw the arrival of new escorts, corvettes or minesweepers, and the departure of the sinister U-boats. The weather thickened and we were sent below. Eventually the engine stopped, and after a while there was a roar and rattle as one anchor was let go. Soon a strange stillness fell on the ship. When allowed on deck for an airing, we could dimly make out the shape of a lighthouse in the mist, which was identified as the one near the mouth of the Gironde river. So, it was to Bordeaux we were bound, we thought.

Down below again, we were not to see the next part of the journey, only listen to the noises and make what we could of them. Link by link the cable clanked home and then there was the familiar shudder as the motor started and the propeller threshed the water. Slow speed ahead; the water ripples gurgled on the bow plating. The pundits told us it was fifty miles from the sea to Bordeaux and that would take some time in this thick weather. She hadn't been under way long before we noticed the speed had been increased. And what was that? We looked at each other questioningly. Did you feel it? No mistake now. The bows were lifting to the Atlantic swell. We weren't going up the river at all. Guessing was rife. Perhaps she was going to St. Nazaire, or Brest. After all, it was argued, KOMET is a part of the Kriegsmarine, so a naval port would be the more likely place to berth her. With these thoughts in mind, we stowed the tables and forms and rigged our hammocks for the night.

In the greyness of 25th November she was still ploughing along, northwards we guessed, but there was no sign of the sun or any other means of our telling the course. And so she continued all day and after nightfall. This was ominous. Could it really be true that they were trying to run up the Channel? Next morning we were in no doubt; allowed on deck, we could see for ourselves as KOMET went through the Channel Islands. It was a brief airing this time, but we did have time to notice that the crew were in life-jackets and fighting rig and that what looked like heavy calibre machine guns had sprouted from the decks all over the place, the most intriguing one being on a platform that could be hoisted on a track up the foremast. This display of weaponry didn't bode well for a quiet afternoon. The noise of the bow wave and the vibration of the hull told us the ship was pressing ahead as fast as the engine could drive the weed-grown bottom through the water. After several hours the tension was relaxed by the sound of the engine stopping, then going astern, followed by the roar of the anchor chain hurtling through the pipes nearby. Where could we be? Eventually allowed on deck, we found ourselves in the harbour of Cherbourg. After taking in the war-dead scene of this great harbour in the fading light of the chilly winter's afternoon, we had nothing else to do than speculate on our fate.

During the night of 26/27th November KOMET got under way again and next morning she was docked in Le Havre. A number of smaller naval craft were there, presumably our escorts. It now seemed inevitable that the Germans would try their luck in a dash through the Dover Strait. Conditions were good for it, long nights and poor visibility. Every one of us had to accept this dreadful prospect as philosophically as his temperament allowed. In fact, I did not see a single man, from the oldest hands to the youngest deck boys and apprentices, show any sign of apprehension – whatever was going on inside him. But it was noticeable that speculation on our fate had now dropped to a very low level. Anyway, there was nothing we could do about it, so we just carried on with our card games, home-made dominoes, Mah-Jong, reading or whatever.

Soon after nightfall we heard the engine kick over and throb into life. Many footfalls, clanks and bumps on the steel decks above told us the crew was at Action Stations. KOMET was soon under way and before long was vibrating under full power. Was this to be another short hop of five or six hours into Dieppe or was it the real thing? Hammocks were rigged and practically everyone turned in – but fully dressed. Ears were alert to every sound. For hours we listened to the rhythmic beat of the engine and the swish of water, until our watches convinced us that it was to be the Strait, or nothing! Suddenly, at 0415, pandemonium broke loose. Staccato bursts of machine-gun fire opened the battle. So at last the Royal Navy had found her, we thought. We prisoners gathered round the companionway exit ready to try to get out quickly and save our lives if possible. The O/C Prisoners had come to the grilled door on the deck and was ready to unlock it in case of sinking. The guns were very noisy. The ammunition hoist running through our door rattled and scraped with activity, and there was no comfort in that reminder of the store of explosives in the hold below us. Judging by the time, we knew we were in the Strait. The gunfire went on and on. In the attacks on KOTA NOPAN and DEVON the salvos were all over in a few minutes, now it was stretching out to an hour. Our nerves began to get tense. The crazy speculation that the Navy might somehow bring KOMET to bay and release us had given place to the more likely probabilities of sudden death by drowning, or a speedier transition to oblivion through the ship being blown up. The stress of the paradox of wanting the 'German bastards' blown to bits but saving our own skins was acute. As a non-smoker I had accumulated a small stock of cigarettes. It was good to see what relief and comfort that store gave to my smoking shipmates who had none of their own left.

Then there was an extra loud bang; the ship suddenly shook and listed to starboard and, at the same time, she swung sharply in that direction. A torpedo hit? The engine was still running. She righted herself and carried on. The firing continued and the ship kept swinging about until 0615. Eventually she slowed down. All went quiet. Soon we knew we were in harbour. It was time for a little sleep.

Later on in the morning we were allowed on deck. What a sight! Shell cases and such debris everywhere. We looked around us. Dunkirk! Unmistakably Dunkirk, with wrecked ships here and there. The harbour installations a shambles. And there were the historic beach and sand dunes stretching away to the east, still littered with the dross of war. The date was 28th November, 1941. We wondered if we were the first Britishers to return. Our mood was almost buoyant; we were all relaxed and smiling after our ordeal. Such was our reaction to the night of tension while we were impotently locked down below. In marked contrast, the Germans were drawn and grim as they cleared the decks. There was not a trace of the homeward bound fever left in them. We laughed at them. No damage to the ship was visible from our viewpoint. they must have suspected that there was some below the waterline further aft, for a diver went down to make an inspection. We had half expected a daylight attack since the Allies must have known that a ship of some importance had fought its way up Channel, but there was no alarm.

KOMET was under way again the same evening. The stress in us all seemed to lessen as the North Sea opened out. There was not another attack so we had a comparatively quiet night. Perhaps this was in part due to the poor visibility we found when let out on deck next morning. Of immediate interest were our escort vessels, which were smallish craft of frigate size or less, and it was with a dash of pride tinged with pleasure that we noticed some bullet holes on some of their superstructures. In mid-afternoon it cleared a little and a pale watery sun shone on us. That spell was just enough for a British reconnaissance aircraft to spot the raider and compel the guards to hustle us down below. KOMET was being pressed ahead at all possible speed. By now we were so familiar with the normal beat of the engine that we were conscious of the change of tempo, just as we noticed the differences in all the other sounds associated with a ship under way, like the swish of the water as the bows clove the calm sea, the creaking rivets and the vibration. There was another sensation that would have been welcome in other circumstances, namely the feel of a ship in shoal water. As we whiled away the rest of the day, shut down below, we had less apprehension of being attacked. Mines worried the more imaginative personalities. I can't say that anyone showed signs of anxiety as we turned in that night, but there was a general awareness that a big change in our lifestyle might take place tomorrow.

We were roused early next morning, Sunday, 30th November, 1941. KOMET was still under way. The orders: stow hammocks, peggies to galley, rig tables and forms, toilet, prepare to disembark after breakfast. Everyone was more or less stirred by the thought of going ashore. My shipmates and I had been at sea for five months all but one week. But it would be a queer pay off this time. We 'enjoyed' our last breakfast, which was a little more substantial than normal. The slice of black bread with a scrape of marge and jam, plus *ersatz* coffee, was supplemented by more of the 'pudding' served yesterday. This was the concoction of dried Australian apple rings from dear old AUSTRALIND's cargo that had pursued us and purged us across three oceans. One felt the Fates were sniggering at this final touch of irony.

About seven o'clock the engine slowed down. Soon KOMET was stopped. At 0715 there was a bang, bang, bang of a hammer on the windlass brake handle, and instantly the cable went clattering out of the hawse-pipe and the anchor bit into German ground. The ship shook as the engine was given a touch astern; more cable was paid out and then she was brought up.

Eventually we were ordered to go on deck with our belongings. When the Officer in charge was satisfied that we all were out, we were marched amidships, then down a gangway on to a tender that was alongside the ship. While this boat took us the short distance to the shore, I looked back at KOMET and a strange mixture of emotions stirred inside me. One can't really hate a ship.

CHAPTER FOUR

Marlag and Milag Nord

There was rime frost glistening in the hazy winter sunshine on the wooden planking of the Cuxhaven landing stage, where the tender had dropped us with our poor baggage. It was a fittingly chilly reception. Captain Hattenboer, at this date rather poorly, was carried on a stretcher and deposited beside us. Strange to say, the frigid landing in this unattractive place did not depress us. On the contrary, in twos and threes we briskly tramped up and down the frosty planking, everyone beaming with smiles like boisterous schoolboys out on a treat. The anxiety of being drowned like caged rats had evaporated. We had room to stretch our legs. What else mattered? To complete the illusion of an outing, four motor coaches arrived for us. But it was a fleeting fancy, for with them came a party of armed men dressed in field grey uniforms. Grim faced Huns they seemed by comparison with the seamen of the Kriegsmarine.

Into the buses we were herded, to be driven to an unknown destination. Aboard KOMET we felt some affinity with her crew; brother seamen just below the skin of war. They had to handle the ship in fair weather and foul, tend her, steer her, navigate her and do all the duties of seamen, engineers and radio men that we ourselves had learnt in the same school over the years. With them on the great oceans we had begun to feel almost at home. All of that world we knew was quickly vanishing, leaving a chill, empty feeling inside.

Now we were being driven across a monotonous fenland in the grip of winter. So this is Germany, real enemy country, cold and inhospitable under a leaden sky! Ahead, and at intervals between the coaches, armed and helmeted guards rode on motorbikes. Their presence was the one bright spot for us in this gloomy cavalcade, for the idea that such an armed escort was necessary for us was so ridiculous that we couldn't help smiling. There was not much to be seen on that bleak landscape save an occasional single-storied farmstead squatting low on the earth as if to keep warm. We passed through no township of any size.

After bumping along the country roads at no great speed for an hour or so, we had the chance of a more intimate look at the scenery. As travellers to the tropical lands will know, the human body in a hot climate gets adjusted to an appropriate level of liquid intake to balance the loss by perspiration. We had spent many months in torrid conditions and now were suddenly plunged into winter weather. There was little enough perspiration on this frosty morning, so we had to demand a halt to be relieved of the surplus liquid in another way. It proved to be an embarrassing occasion for us young men unaccustomed to 'continental' habits, for just as we stood lined up facing the ditch, a group of young women came cycling past. And we hadn't seen a woman for months. I'm afraid we didn't notice the scenery after all.

We must have been on the road for the better part of three hours when the outriders swung right into a lane, and soon the coaches were brought to a halt alongside a tall, barbed-wire fence. Peering out through the steamy windows, we saw a few men behind the fence dressed in French Army uniform jackets and queer nondescript headgear. We guessed they were foreigners. This is it! We have arrived!

We remained stationery for a while on the outside of that fence. Of course, as one soon learns, prisoners can take no initiative in such situations. It's – Wait here! Do this! Don't do that! In due course someone had taken the necessary action to get the gate opened and the convoy admitted to the prison camp. Armed sentries were posted at the entrance. All hands had to disembark just inside the gate, now significantly closed and locked, and were ushered into a nearby wooden barrack which appeared to be a large mess room or hall. The time was about two o'clock in the afternoon.

German naval personnel sat at tables disposed about the hall and we were ordered to present ourselves at one and the other in turns. Then started the slow process of recording our personal particulars, even our religion, and, of course, a finger print of the right index finger. All these data were duly written down on a card, one for each man. In this process everyone was given a number, mine was 21, and at the same time received a sheet-metal tally, size 2⅞" x 1⅝". On this tally was embossed – MARLAG + MILAG NORD Kgf Nr. 21. Curiously, this legend was repeated, upside down, on the same face of the plate. Furthermore, there were thin slotted perforations right across the tally, dividing the two texts; only six small pieces of metal held the two parts together. One of these halves had a ⅛" round hole at each end, the other half had but one such hole at one end. We learned that in the event of death, the tally would be broken into two pieces. The piece with the two holes would be screwed on to the coffin, the other would be hung up on a hook or nail in the office as a record. Each man was issued with a shallow brown enamelled bowl, a mug of a similar dingy hue, a shoddy alloy spoon, two dark-coloured blankets that were none too thick, and a coarse unbleached linen sheet. With due solemnity we were ordered to acknowledge the receipt of this bounty by signing appropriate documents. Finally, to the accompaniment of shouted commands, boot stamping, heel clicking and answering cries of 'jawohl' from the guards, we picked up our few belongings – minus watches, knives and such *verboten* objects – and were marched to Barrack No. 19, in the part aptly named 'Siberia'.

Entering the wooden building by the door in its end, we found it had a central alleyway running the whole of its length, with doors on each side leading into the fourteen rooms. Although we did not appreciate it at that instant, we were being introduced to the stereotype of countless thousands of such barracks that were the 'homes' of hundreds of thousands throughout the Greater Reich. The rooms were filled with pairs of wooden bunks, one atop the other; a table and a few benches. There was a window in the outside wall, and in an inside corner a closed stove – known as a 'bogie' by old-time 'salts'. Somebody had thoughtfully started a fire in it and provided a bucket of briquettes. Home at last! Each man chose a bunk in the room to which he was allotted – or took the remnant if slow off the mark – and dumped his gear on it. With these simple formalities completed and the guards withdrawn, we took up our newly-acquired tableware and were conducted to the Mess Room. About a third of this hut was occupied as a galley, the remainder was an open 'hall'. It was here that we were treated to our first taste of camp food. The cooks, we heard, had arranged a special 'sitting' for

The Milag Nord Camp

My Identity Card

us. It was a nondescript soup in which the only recognizable ingredient, at this stage of our education, was potato – in a few small pieces. But it was hot, and having had nothing since our early breakfast on KOMET, we were very hungry by late afternoon and glad to get it, whatever it was. Mercifully, we were not then made aware that there was seldom anything else on the menu. We were now free to communicate with the other residents of the camp[1]. This was a heart-warming experience. We quickly discovered that, in spite of their unconventional rig, they were Allied Merchant Navy personnel, mostly British, plus a few civilian passengers taken from ships. They were anxious to gather news of the outside world and took us into their rooms to talk. They brewed tea for us on the bogie. Real English tea. What a luxury after nearly four months of *'ersatz'*! Smokers enjoyed 'Player's' and 'Goldflake' that were handed out with great generosity. How on earth did you get hold of these? We then heard of the work of the Red Cross, that splendid organization that could save our lives and preserve our sanity, given an adequate degree of co-operation by the German authorities. 'Do they co-operate?' 'Well, we suspect they are lukewarm about forwarding the food parcels from Switzerland, for deliveries are erratic. Often there have been long gaps. But they seem to have improved a bit. Rumour has it that we shall receive a consignment within a few days, so you might be lucky.'

We trickled back to our barrack aglow with the warmth of the friendship of our new-found camp-mates. Now we had to get ourselves sorted out before lights-out. The mattress sacks, made of a coarse-woven *'ersatz'* yarn, had been crudely filled with wood-shavings, and not a few lumps of wood that had to be moved to one side for comfort. It was evident that the roof of this recently-erected old hut leaked, for my mattress was wet. I took the precautions I could to minimize the effect of this by laying my uniform raincoat, which was once fairly waterproof, on the mattress and under the blanket. And so, at the end of the most eventful day since our

---

[1] *Later admissions to the camp were usually kept in isolation until they all had been subjected to interrogation by German officers at Wilhelmshaven or, later, at Marlag + Milag Nord itself. So this was another benefit we enjoyed, though we did not recognize it at the time.*

capture, the light was dowsed and we all turned in. It proved to be one of the most miserable nights I could remember, cold to the marrow of my bones and utterly uncomfortable. Soreness gripped my throat and I knew that heralded a cold on the chest. If only I could sleep!

With the dawn of 1st December, 1941, there started our initiation into the drab routine that was to mould our lives for years to come. A German guard came into the barrack shouting, *'Reise, reise, austehen!'* and banged doors with his rifle butt to emphasize his message. My limbs were stiff and numb as I tumbled out of my upper bunk to dress. The clothes that I hadn't kept on me overnight were clammy. And my uniform suit (tailor-made by one of Sydney's best tailors only six months before), that had just served as an auxiliary blanket, looked as depressed as I felt. I was putting my paper-thin shoes on as the guard returned bawling, *'Raus, raus, appel, appel'*. The 'bell' rang (it was a couple of feet of iron girder, hung by a wire on a kind of gibbet and struck by a bar) and we shambled off to the large parade ground, or *platz*, for our first *appel*[1] in the half-light of this winter dawn. It was raw and misty, the temperature fortunately above freezing. Prisoners were assembled in Barrack groups in rows, three deep. *'Drei und drei'* were the new words we had to learn and were supposed to obey. 'Our' guard counted us. Then crossly re-counted, for we had moved about a bit without regard to his fumbling efforts to achieve the correct tally. Then he stood at ease nearby till the sergeant came. Heel clicks, arm up – *'Heil Hitler, sechs und neunzig'*. *'Heil Hitler,'* the sergeant answered and began to count us himself. *'Drei und drei,'* the guard bawled in self-defence, when he noticed our sloppy line up. We eyed the counter closely as he made his tally. A burly fellow in 'field grey'. Was this the infamous Feldwebel Rompa we heard about last night? Just as dampness from the wet sand (a mercy it wasn't clay) had percolated through my soles, the sergeant finished his count of us, the last barrack. 'You vill not talk,' he hissed as he made his total and then strode ostentatiously into the centre of the *platz*. In a voice beloved of his kind he bellowed, *'Achtung'*. Heels

---

[1] *Appel = muster for counting.*

clicked. Prisoners shuffled more or less into line and stood still. A tall, thin figure in the uniform of the Kriegsmarine approached from the gate. He wore the rings of a Captain on his cuffs and a short sword dangled from his belt. When he was some ten feet from him, the sergeant's heels clicked like a pistol shot, his right arm shot up at an angle of 45° as he rasped out, *'Heil Hitler'*. *'Heil Hitler,'* was the tired reply. There was an audible exchange between the two, though unintelligible to us. Presumably it meant 'all present and correct' for, after further saluting, *'der Kapitan'* made his exit. The sergeant picked out a few men for working parties and the whole performance was over inside twenty minutes when he ordered, 'Dees-mees'. Some old hands came over and congratulated us. 'You must have had a good influence on the old bastard. We haven't had such a short *appel* for weeks. Keep it up!'

After this ritual the peggy appointed for our room made his way to the galley with the enamelled ewer and bowl provided (both in the same tasteful chocolate colour), to draw the room's quota of *ersatz* coffee and the day's ration of black bread, margarine and jam. Then began our standard breakfast – one or two thin slices out of five that could be cut from a man's ration, thinly smeared with marge and jam, and washed down with the familiar brown fluid. Of course, one could indulge in more than two slices, but such gluttony would leave less for the remainder of the day. The great advantage that careful housekeepers could claim for this regime was that one could always maintain the standard, and not start the day with a gastronomic disappointment.

We had heard with relief of some of the good work of the International Red Cross Society, such as the food parcels, and we were also told about P.O.W. mail. Like the rest of KOMET's contingent, I was eager to let the dear ones at home know that I was alive and well. It was painful to think that they had already endured the anxiety of the uncertainty of our fate for three months. So it was a great event to be issued with a postcard on which the happy message could be written on that December 1st, with the fervent hope that it would get home by Christmas. We were told that each man was allowed to send four cards and three letters a month. The cards held only seven five-inch lines and the letters twenty-four. No doubt their severe limitations were a boon to pen-chewers at a loss for words, and they concentrated the mind of those tending to prolixity. It also cheered us to know that we could receive (at least in theory) any number of letters, one clothing parcel a quarter, parcels of cigarettes without restriction and book parcels. Nobody had the heart to tell us that an exchange of correspondence took four to five months.

To be able to take more than nineteen paces in any one direction was in itself a novelty and a pleasure, so at the earliest opportunity we newcomers indulged in walks of exploration and exercise about the camp. As compared with life aboard KOMET we felt we had entered a new world, more spacious and safer, peopled with our own countrymen or allies and where we could talk more freely. Yet the 12-foot high double fence of barbed wire, with machine-guns and searchlights mounted in high watch towers at each corner, brought home to us that we were now prisoners in enemy territory much more emphatically than did our confinement on the raider.

The campsite sloped gently to the south. There were farmlands towards the east and the south and spiky-topped pinewoods in the distance. On the north side one could see a house and we learnt that beyond the trees in that direction lay the nearby village of Westertimke. There was more activity and interest on the west side. First, there was the fascinating 'Gate', the sole entrance to and exit from the camp. It was always guarded by an armed sentry. In that first December, with winter creeping over us, there was little to stimulate the hope of ever getting out of it. The camp road ran between 'the wire' and fir trees beyond. Opposite the gate was the Kommandant's office and a few other buildings. To the south-west, over open ground, stood Marlag, the camp for R.N. prisoners, under the same German administration, just visible but out of earshot. In many ways the most interesting sight for us was a small, single-storied, timber-framed farmhouse, old and weathered. It stood on the other side of the camp road and on the village side of the Kommandant's office. I supposed it was attractive because it was a real home, and as it was in full view we seemed to get to know the inhabitants, the principal one of which was an elderly woman known to us all as Ma *Arbeit* (Old Mother Work). Other houses near the village, though in our view, did not

Barrack 15

Glimpse of Hospital from Room 3, Barrack 15

attract the same attention[1].

The main feature of the camp was the *'Platz'* or Parade Ground; a cheerless place some 100 yards by 80 yards in size. This is where all hands were mustered for counting, at this stage of the camp's development. Apart from the gate opening directly on to it, there were barracks arranged on all four sides of the *platz* and some of them quickly assumed importance in our lives. There was the Parcels Office with a crude post box hung upon it, both of which came to have vital practical and emotional significance for us. There was the Wash Room, with long metal troughs fitted with cold water sprinklers at intervals and some cold showers for the ultra hardy or 'health cranks'; in all respects strictly utilitarian with no hint of beauty in their design or construction. Between Barracks 5 and 7 at the far end of the square one glimpsed another building, Barrack 6, the infamous communal latrine, noisome in warm weather and brutally cold and draughty in winter. Periodically the contents of its cesspit were pumped into a cylindrical tank mounted on a horse-drawn wagon, 'Smelly Nelly', and removed from the camp. On a winter's day there was nothing about the place to inspire hope or elevate the spirit; just gloom and depression.

By midday we were feeling a bit peckish and were glad when we could queue up at the galley with our bowls, present our *'Esskarte'* for stamping (a personal food-ration card) and receive a ladle of soup. We soon discovered there was a great day-to-day similarity in the insipidity of the Milag brew as compared with that on KOMET. In the latter it must be conceded there were to be found Oriental ingredients to excite the curiosity, even if they did not tickle the palate. Now we could savour the *'kartoffelen'* (potatoes) and, served separately, either mashed swede, turnips or sauerkraut.

To re-assure us of their desire for our continued presence our hosts had another get-together on the *platz* in the evening, and we had our second lesson forming ranks *'drei und drei'*. After which it was peggies to the galley for *ersatz* tea to help down a slice or whatever proportion of our day's ration of bread, marge and jam we had been

---

[1]*Matting was attached to the barbed wire fence at a later date to obscure our view on this side of the camp.*

continent enough to save for the evening 'meal'.

Lights out was at 10.30 p.m.

Our captors observed the distinction between officers and ratings – perhaps that was part of the Geneva Convention concerning Prisoners of War – a document we never saw. The only practical effects of this were that Masters, Mates, Engineers and Radio Officers were not compelled to go on working parties either in or outside the camp, and they were segregated in their own barracks. The Captains, Chief Engineers and certain other 'Barrack Captains' had the privilege of living in 'end rooms', housing only two men, of which there were four to each barrack. Otherwise the same treatment was meted out to all hands.

Because of this policy of segregation, I and other newly arrived officers were soon transferred to Barrack 15. This was an empty hut located in that, roughly, one-third part of the camp which lay to the north of the *platz*. Personally, I was glad of the move, for there were a few fir trees and oak scrub dotted about which reduced the harshness of the scene. The window of my Room 3 faced west and overlooked the Hospital barrack. This was to be my home for a long time.

In the alley-way running straight through the middle of the barrack from end to end were wooden lockers, each allocated to two men to house any spare clothing, other belongings and, when we had it, foodstuffs not consumed at the previous meal. On top of them was an assortment of containers ranging from suitcases such as I was lucky enough to have salvaged from my ship, to Red Cross cartons. And they contained a strange assortment of things, useful like a spare shirt, or desirable like books, and strange odds and ends that 'might come in handy'. In time one might acquire a padlock to safeguard one's treasurers (that were not secreted in one's bunk, the one nearly sacrosanct spot that could be called one's own). The Germans had access to every place and it was only by cunning that anything could be hidden from them.

The size and furnishings of rooms in Barrack 15 were identical with all the rest in the camp. The dimensions were 8 metres by 5 metres. There were 16 (or 18) bunks 2m by 3/4m arranged in pairs one above another; a table of the same dimensions; a couple of forms and some four-legged stools; a 'bogie' for heating stood in one corner.

There was one door leading into the central alleyway and a window about about 1½m by 1½m on the outer wall that looked on to the 'Krankenhaus', i.e. the hospital. All was of bare deal except the four-legged stools, which were of beechwood. As to how grim or how tolerable this spartan accommodation was depended on several factors. The number of men and the weather were basic considerations. Eighteen men in wet, cold weather day after day, with nowhere else to go, were not conducive to comfort, even by camp standards. A reduction of just two bunks some months later came as a great relief.

The most important factor was the character of the inmates. Were they clean and tidy; not loud-mouthed chatterboxes; thoughtful of others and willing to do the communal chores; were they cheerful and not unduly given to fits of depression; were they naturally tolerant; did they want to make the best of Zimmer No. 3? Possession of these traits would not necessarily mean that your soul mate was in the room, he or other kindred spirits might well live in another barrack, but without these attributes in fair measure, bad could be made intolerably worse.

Apart from the separation of officers from the ratings, ships' crews did tend to get split up in the process of finding accommodation for all hands. But to Room 3 were allocated six from AUSTRALIND and a like quota from DEVON, and in this period of transition it was good to have old shipmates about one. Let it be said of our merchant seamen that the nature of their calling, and the life and conditions at sea in those days, bred men of resource, tolerance and adaptability, ideally suited to making the best of captivity. When considering these aspects of life in Milag, it should be remembered that rank had little significance. Master, Mates and Engineers did not have the same authority over the crews as did officers and N.C.O.s in the other services. It is therefore to the greater credit of those men, both officers and ratings, who by their natural abilities became the initiators and leaders of the many healthy activities that were developed.

We soon discovered that Marlag and Milag Nord was a new prison camp, born it seemed of the rivalry between the German fighting services. The pride of the Kriegsmarine craved the custody of the prisoners it had captured. So, in early September, 1941, Pat

Brady, a Radio Officer of PORT HOBART and a party of twenty ratings, were singled out at random from the ranks at *appel* in the camp Stalag XB at Sandbostel and marched under six armed guards to the village of Westertimke, a distance of some 30km. Nearby were several barracks among a scattering of fir trees, originally intended to house Luftwaffe personnel operating an airfield to be built on the clearing to the south. Apparently the site was found to be unsuitable for that purpose and abandoned. German efficiency? The task of the pioneering party, ironically, was to erect the barbed wire fence around the site to keep them in. Nevertheless, the semi-natural setting with its scent of pine trees and long grass was a welcome change from the desolation of Sandbostel, where Russian prisoners in the adjoining compound were callously starved to death.

Pat recalled flushing a partridge from the undergrowth one day. Borrowing a knife from a friendly guard, he had made a bow and arrows and stalked the game in earnest, much to the amusement of the Germans. And in the course of a fortnight he bagged one bird and a red squirrel.

Subsequently parties of men arrived at intervals from Sandbostel, and from Wultzburg Castle which had also held a number of merchant seamen, to populate the new camp.

When we arrived, there were nearly 2,000 old hands there who were applying their talents to creating a tolerable mode of existence.

Everyone had his personal story of capture and adventure before landing in Milag. Somewhat like the brave Cockneys in the London blitz who wore a badge saying, 'I don't want to know about your bomb', there was a hesitancy to say much about one's own experiences. Inevitably, facts did emerge and those of us who had made the long voyage aboard KOMET soon realized that we had cause to be thankful for Vice-Admiral Eyssen and his tactics of daylight attacks. True, we had lost our fine young Captain and two other shipmates, and AUSTRALIND herself, but some raider commanders, we learned, stalked their unsuspecting victims from afar in daylight, then, under cover of darkness, closed in on them to open fire with guns and/or torpedoes. This was a fate only better than a U-boat attack in that one's chance of survival after a sinking was greater. To their credit, raider commanders seldom failed to rescue survivors even at risk to themselves. It had been our good fortune, too, that we had not been absolutely overcrowded in the prisoners' accommodation on the raider. We had not endured the appalling conditions some had suffered in the holds of supply ships or prizes on the way 'home' to Europe.

We also learned what a dreadful overland journey from Bordeaux we had missed by our passage up Channel on KOMET.

And now, though they were early days to judge, the hope was that the *Kriegsmarine* at Marlag and Milag Nord would prove to be kindlier janitors than the *Wehrmacht* had been elsewhere.

The arrival of a consignment of Red Cross food parcels was heartening. I gladly complied with a request to sign a special postcard confirming that I, *Kriegsgefangen* 21, had received my first parcel that day, 12th December, 1941. That card went to the Red Cross and I suppose got my name put on their files: I certainly hoped so. After living four months on only stomach-inflating slops, it was a thrill hard to describe, to see, and then enjoy, really good British foodstuffs; all labelled with familiar brand names too. Spirits soared and did so again when I received another parcel before Christmas.

The receipt of these parcels posed the problem of how we new boys should organize ourselves in order to utilize them to best advantage. Already we had tips from old hands that it was better to band together in 'combines' and pool and share out the food rather than each man sticking to his own box. This was especially advantageous when tinned meats could be extended by mixing their contents with the German potato ration to make hash and such dishes. Compatability of taste and temperament, within a combine, was important for the preservation of peace. Pairing was popular with us, but one did hear of quite large combines. I was fortunate in teaming up with John Andrews, a canny young Scottish engineer from DEVON. Both of us could restrain our appetites and not gobble up everything at once, however hungry we might be. Our motto, 'Keep a wee bit in the locker', stood us in good stead in lean times, for there were occasions when others were starving yet we had a little of something. We never fell out over menus. Jock was a great combine mate.

Luckily the weather in December was fairly mild, for a good

many of us lacked clothing and footwear suitable for winter conditions in Germany. Although I was better off than some others, for Mr. Strickers, the Chief Officer of KOTA NOPAN, had kindly supplemented my tropical rig with warmer underwear, morning *appels* struck chill in my under-nourished body. We were dreading a cold spell but at the psychological moment the Germans made some clothing available. It was obviously loot originating from France. I received one of those blue and white striped matelot vests and a pair of thick blue cloth trousers, the sort with a big flap at the front that takes a bit of managing when one is in a hurry! An old Polish army jacket completed the rig. For footwear I received old army boots, one French, the other Polish. At least they weren't a bad fit and they looked waterproof. By some mismanagement, or through a wry sense of humour, our outfitters did not supply boot laces. Style was of no consequence and one thought little about the former owners or of their fate. So, in our new rig we blended in better with the native fauna, but it was to be a long time before we had the luxury of a British battle dress, or the comfort of an army great coat.

Soon after this Moss Bros. act we were ordered to spruce ourselves up to be photographed. This was done mostly in room groups with the promise that we would each be able to buy a copy. Immediately afterwards we were photographed again, each holding his P.O.W. number, as a little memento for our hosts.

There were two faintly amusing sequels to my sessions in front of the camera. The Germans ultimately tumbled to the fact that a photo of a bearded man was of doubtful value in their security archives. So I was ordered to shave and be re-photographed. I wasn't keen on that, for I had got used to wearing a beard. It was warmer and one avoided the worry of procuring razor blades and the agony of shaving with old blunt edges in difficult conditions. It must have been the kindly Dr. Blanck who dealt with the matter, for on the pretext that I was taking part in a forthcoming play (only one of the rabble in the 'Vagabond King') I was allowed to keep it until the show was over. The Teutonic god of Order and Efficiency was placated by issuing me with a *'Bart Karte'* (Beard Card), authorizing me to keep my beard for the prescribed period, after which I had to be photographed again, clean-shaven. The second was rather more touching than amusing. My dear mother evidently examined the photo with great care under a magnifying glass and noticed my boots were laced with string. It was, in fact, the thick near-white string used on Red Cross food parcels. Some months later, good leather bootlaces appeared in my first clothing parcel. Bless her dear heart!

CHAPTER FIVE

Dual Control

Our new hosts constantly surrounded us, were frequently in our midst and continually influenced our existence, for better or worse. On the raider we had been accustomed to seeing Germans, real Germans, the enemy, the authors of our misfortune and miseries. But, to be truthful, they had not corresponded at all closely to the arrogant, heel-clicking, goose-stepping types we had seen in films in the pre-war years and had been reminded of constantly in the Allied news and propaganda. Granted, we had little close contact with them, but we had the distinct impression they bore us no personal animosity. Certainly there had been no bullying, let alone ill-treatment. I don't mean we were exactly pleased with our lot, or that we felt the urge to give three cheers for KOMET and her gallant crew when we left her; nevertheless, we now perceived that, by comparison, we had to accommodate ourselves to a different breed of gaolers, something more like the true *Herrenvolk*.

One had only to get a glimpse of Kommandant Schuur, the man in charge of the whole Marlag and Milag Nord complex, to realize that the *Kriegsmarine* were not devoting the finest flower of their manpower to taking care of us. It looked as if this undersized Prussian, with goatee beard, had been taken off the retirement shelf, dusted and put into a bright uniform. I heard no good spoken of him, but had no personal contact with him myself, to verify that reputation. He was known to us as 'Poopdeck Pappy'.

The person who more directly influenced our lives was his underling responsible for Milag, Kapitan Prusch, alias 'Sauerkraut'. To us, standing on *appel* with empty bellies in the cold, this nickname seemed to sum up aptly this gaunt, hatchet-faced specimen of a resurrected one-time naval officer. He became the focus of all our pent-up venom and even real hatred of all things Teutonic that afflicted us. His mere presence seemed to exude cantankerous nastiness which affected all hands, including the German guards.

Two views of the Milag Nord Camp

There were times on unnecessarily prolonged *appels* in the first bitter winter when I, normally easy going and slow to anger, would have gladly shot him dead if I had had a gun, and taken the consequences.

To execute his will and to make things tick, or should I say 'click', Sauerkraut had the services of Feldwebel Rompa, a big, boisterous, bullying under-officer. He was the scourge of the German lower ranks. He did his worst to instil and maintain a degree of good order among us prisoners on parade by bluff and the power to inflict the discomforts of cold and wet by prolonging *appels*. And he could put any recalcitrants on to a *'strafegang'* or other unpleasant working party. He did, however, display occasionally a trait that was rather more endearing. Unlike any other German we encountered, he had a rough sense of humour which he was pleased to regale us with in public. In his English, which was quite good (rumour had it that he had worked in a shipping office in the U.K.) he would admonish new arrivals: 'You see zee barbed vire fence, ja? Eet iss to keep you in. We do not like you to leave us. Andt you see zee single vire one metre from zee groundt, drei meter fon zee fence, ja? You shall not jump ofer eet. Eet is not for your washing to hang on. Eet iss not zee Siegfried Line. Eet iss zee varning vire. Eef you step ofer eet zee vachtman will shoot you dead. You understand?'

Our more intimate contacts with our captors were with the guards. We called them all *'posten'*, whether in the singular or plural, and regardless of the duty they were performing. Like Rompa, and his much pleasanter deputy Vollman, they wore the field-grey uniform of the army. For the most part they were relatively elderly men, though there was a sprinkling of youngsters in their ranks when we came to the camp. Some appeared to be C3, or the equivalent German health grade.

They manned the machine guns and searchlights on the four watch-towers; stood sentry at the gate; tramped their beats outside the wire at night, steel helmeted and armed, winter and summer; others patrolled inside the camp after lights-out, sometimes with dogs. But it was in their capacity as *Barraken Führer* (one guard allocated to each barrack to ensure we turned out for *appel*, etc.) or as *Arbeit Posten* (working party guards) that we took a special interest in them. Although generally ignorant of one another's language, we studied them closely and sought to know their characters. This was not in general for the purpose of friendly intercourse, but specifically to discover any weakness or other attribute that could be exploited to our advantage. Weaknesses there were and they were exploited.

On the whole, Barrack Guards wanted a trouble-free life with us prisoners on the one hand, and especially with Rompa & Co. on the other. Their greatest fear was of being transferred to the Eastern Front so it was highly desirable to keep their noses clean. Their dread increased in proportion with bad news and high casualty figures from the Russian Front. I am afraid we had no mercy on them and would raise this bogey when a guard was in a barrack alone if we wanted to bait him. It was a cruel sport.

There were, however, some guards, good natured men who had no more stomach for Hitler's war than we had, with whom good relations were discreetly cultivated. Through them business was done in eggs, the odd knife or small hand tool in exchange for cigarettes. In a few instances we were forewarned of a camp search so that *'verboten'* articles could be the better secreted.

The *Arbeits Posten* occupied a position of considerable importance for us, for they and the working parties of prisoners in their charge, constituted the main channel of trade between us and the outside world. A 'good' guard was one lax in the finer points of military discipline, generally a non-Nazi, and one who didn't set too high a price on his conscience.

There was one gentleman whose life's work was to thwart any such irregularities and much more beside. Herr Güsfeld, local functionary of the loathsome Gestapo, exercised his baleful influence throughout the camp and its neighbourhood. This pink-faced creature with steely eyes, had a big nose, purpose-made it seemed, for detecting the slightest whiff of contraband, be it a couple of plover's eggs, a pocket compass or an illicit radio receiver. He operated the whole censorship apparatus covering the camp. All incoming letters and parcels were scrutinized by his minions and stamped *'Geprüft'*. Outgoing mail, naturally, received identical treatment. To us he represented the quintessence of Nazism. We believed his suspicious mind would detect a sinister motive in a baby's cry for a nappy change. He was universally detested. Whilst I personally doubt the rumour that he sometimes had prisoners' mail deliberately burnt, there is no question about the truth of a dirty frame-up he perpetrated on a Belgian officer. Güsfeld barged into this man's room and went straight over to his bunk and rummaged in the bedding. Within seconds he produced a revolver and confronted the bewildered man with it. He was immediately arrested and taken from the camp. We never knew why this dastardly trick had been played, nor what became of the poor fellow. At the time it left us with a feeling of nauseating helplessness. Yes, Herr Güsfeld was an ever-present and insidious menace. However, he was also a challenge to us to match cunning with greater cunning, search with even more ingenious concealment. It was his wits against ours.

It should be remembered that when we arrived in Europe at the end of 1941 the Germans had scored great military and naval successes and were in a triumphant mood. They were arrogantly confident they would soon bomb Britain into submission, overrun Russia and hoist the swastika over half the world; this was reflected in their hard attitude towards us.

Whilst this phalanx of the *Herrenvolk* generally set the limits of our existence, the details of our daily lives were largely in our own hands. The formal channel of communication between the Germans and ourselves was through the Camp Captain, known officially as the Man of Confidence. This latter title was a significant one for it was necessary for the holder of the office to enjoy the confidence of the parties on each side of the wire if he were to be in the least effective. It demanded a strong personality with plenty of common sense and not a little diplomacy to firmly represent our hetero-national interests to the Germans and to interpret and get acceptance of any unpleasant orders or responses that came from them. In neighbouring Marlag, where Royal Navy discipline prevailed, it must have been a somewhat easier task. However, Merchant Navy Ship-Masters and Officers were accustomed to commanding respect and obedience by strength of character reacting on the general good sense of their crews. The 'Articles' gave them little support. Captain Lewis was our first spokesman. He was unsparing in his efforts for the prisoners' welfare and stood up to the authorities. In the end the Germans must have thought this gun-running Skipper of the Spanish civil war too inflexible to merit their confidence, for others succeeded him. Captain Notman did this tightrope act with distinction for the final two years of the war.

Each barrack had a Barrack Captain whose duty it was to ensure that good order and cleanliness were maintained. In spite of the title, the office holder might have been of any rank or rating. Again, strength of character and tact were the essential qualifications. A burly physique and an accomplished rough-house manner were also useful attributes. These men had a certain liaison with the Barrack Guards in getting us on to *appel* in good time and in other 'domestic' matters. For their trouble they were privileged to live in an 'end room' with only one other occupant.

As the *appels* passed in monotonous procession and December 25th approached, it was interesting to notice the change in mood that came about amongst the prisoners, and even the guards. Rooms were decorated with gay-coloured paper chains created out of labels off the Red Cross food tins and sprigs of fir, snatched from the camp trees. Strange to say, a festive spirit began to pervade the drab place.

Late on Christmas Eve carol singing was heard around the camp. There was a haunting beauty about the strains of 'Silent Night', sung in harmony, as they floated over the still midnight air. And one thought of other Christmases and loved ones outside the beastly wire, away over the North Sea.

Breakfast was up to standard: *ersatz* coffee, two thin slices of black bread with a meagre scrape of marge and jam. The weather was dry and rather mild. The *appel* was short. It was 'Happy Christmas, Happy Christmas' all around.

There was a non-denominational carol service in the hall mid-morning and many attended it.

The cooks did a wonderful job, with food pooled from Red Cross parcels, in producing a Christmas dinner far out of the ordinary run of camp menus, though in a letter home I did comment that 'by chance the turkeys weren't delivered'.

The second *appel* too was mercifully short. At tea we even had a few cakes and mince pies that the cooks had somehow managed to make out of pounded Red Cross biscuits, oatmeal and dried fruit; another welcome break in the monotony of our diet in the last four months.

Our extraordinary day was rounded off with a pantomime, Aladdin's Lamp, performed in the dining hall, with music by the 'Orama' band. This took our minds right off the war, food and the future; and it opened our eyes to the talent latent in these strangely clad fellows we were gradually coming to know. Life could be a lot worse.

There was a brave attempt to greet the New Year with a smile, but that was a gesture of irrational hope, as far from reality as the 'near beer' we drank was from a good brew. (The Germans had sold us a small ration of this *ersatz* beer.) There was little enough to look back on with pleasure in the Old Year. 'Lord Haw-Haw', the traitor, braying out daily over the camp's one loud-speaker, was now our main source of news. In our short time in Milag he had drooled over the almost incredible report of Pearl Harbour on December 7th, and the equally incredible sinking of the battleships, PRINCE OF WALES and REPULSE, on the 10th. Now this unctuous voice was asking us to believe that Hong Kong had fallen to the Japanese on Christmas Day, and our Dutch friends to swallow bitter news from the East Indies. His proclivity for exaggeration and lying were so well known, and this catalogue so great, that we didn't believe him. Unhappily for once he spoke the truth; and when this was eventually verified we could see little of comfort ahead in the New Year, save the entry of the United States into the war on our side. It was a dismal and depressing prospect.

Within a week, as if conspiring with the enemy to break our morale, the wind veered round to the east. And it blew from that quarter without intermission until the end of March, bringing with it straight from Siberia a succession of bone-chilling blizzards. Snow built up about the camp and the temperature fell lower and lower. Water vapour from our breath condensed and froze on the inside of the window until the ice was a good inch thick.

The supply of Red Cross parcels failed just when we needed extra food to counteract the low temperature, for it goes without saying that we had no reserves of fat to draw upon. For a time we had to put up with the arctic conditions of *appel* on the *platz* twice a day on empty bellies, until even the well-clad Germans relented and made the counts in the barrack alleyways.

When a peggy went out first thing into the drifting snow to get the 'coffee' he reminded one exactly of the painting of Captain Scott's self-sacrificing companion, Captain Oates, stepping out into the storm to his death.

There was little we could do in these conditions save huddle in our rooms with everything battened down, play cards or board games, or read if you were lucky enough to have the games or books, and just then many hadn't. Keeping the bogey burning fast enough to maintain a tolerable temperature on a minimum of fuel consumption was an art we had to learn quickly. For in the extreme conditions lack of fuel soon became a problem. The ration of briquettes was not sufficient. It was in this crisis that our Norwegian room-mate, Einar Naess, spotted the fuel potential of the cinders mixed in the clinkers that formed the surface of some of the paths of the camp. So cinder-picking became a worthwhile, if disagreeable, communal activity which helped to keep the stove alight at a time of great need.

Our one consolation, and that a perverse one, was that, bleak as it was here, it must be even worse for the Germans fighting around Stalingrad. It was our uncharitable wish, expressed in unrefined nautical laughter, that the lot of them might freeze to death.

In the grim weeks ahead, food, and the lack of it, became the obsessive topic of conversation. In four months of captivity we had, by experience, come to appreciate the minimum level of nourishment necessary for survival. Old Sandbostel hands underlined this with accounts of the ghastly effects of the basic German ration on Russian prisoners who were compelled to labour on it. Sandbostel was a composite prison camp embracing several compounds separated only by barbed wire fences. At one stage (1940-41) Russian prisoners were next to the Merchant Navy, so many of our immediate comrades saw the appallingly inhuman treatment to which these poor creatures were subjected. It was heart-rending to see gangs of them returning from labour outside the camp, slouching back to their barracks emaciated in body and broken in spirit, and not be able to help them in any way for communication was *'strengt verboten'*. Deaths among the Russians were frequent, and as a barrack in view of the British prisoners was used as a mortuary, they could not help seeing from time to time naked bodies taken from it and unceremoniously piled up in carts and taken away for mass burial.

Chapter Six

The Third Degree

In mid-January, when the Easterly blizzard had settled down to a continuous moan in the fir trees and our whole world was frozen solid, an order came that we new arrivals were to be transported to the German Naval base at Wilhelmshafen for interrogation. We contemplated this trip with misgiving. Apart from the weather conditions, we were apprehensive about what sort of pressure might be applied to us to obtain information.

As it happened, we were taken in groups and my party did not go until 10th February, 1942, by which time we had some assurance from those who had been examined that our captors treated them gently. I, personally was glad of that news because I had a good deal of information, quite unconnected with the sea, that the Germans would wish to extort if they only knew it resided in my memory.

Of course, the mere idea of getting out of the camp, even under armed guard had a certain fascination and excitement about it. But there was no doubt we were in for a chilly journey. We put on the warmest clothing we could muster and stuffed the minimal toilet requisites in our pockets.

With the usual rough shouts to urge us on, we clambered into a canvas-covered military truck with an ample quota of armed guards. We bumped out of the camp and jolted and swayed along the wintry roads. There was nothing to see or do save hang on to avoid injury or frostbite from the frigid blasts blowing through the cracks. Luckily it was only three miles to Tarmstedt. There we found a funny little narrow-gauge train waiting, in a primitive station. It wasn't a 'prisoners only' special. Much to our interest, there were Germans travelling too. A few were military personnel but they mostly looked like local farming people on their way to town shopping. All were well wrapped up with little of their faces showing, and they seemed intent on their own business and took no notice of us.

In other circumstances that little steam train would have

commanded considerable attention; as it was, we were hustled into compartments on our own as quickly as possible, with no opportunity of contact with the civilians. Huddled together on the hard wooden seats, we kept one another warm as the Lilliputian loco hauled us the fifteen miles or so to Bremen.

The guards hemmed us in as we disembarked, lined us up on the platform and counted us. Then we were marched through the subways, out on to side streets, traipsing along in the gutters to the main-line station. This was a strange experience, for it was the first time that any of us had been in a built-up township for seven months, added to which this was enemy territory. Our eyes were sharp to notice any sign of war damage, but we didn't see much to gloat over. The civilians who passed displayed no interest in us, though our appearance, I thought, could only provoke contempt or pity. Once on the appropriate platform in the *Hauptbahnhof*, the guards kept us well away from the populace and again counted us. Overawed by the weather and in poor physical condition to withstand it, no-one felt the urge to slip into the crowd if the chance came.

The main-line train was heated and it carried us to Wilhelmshafen in comparative comfort, but the steamed up windows gave little opportunity for spying the enemy countryside.

Shambling along the streets of Wilhelmshafen, and now being stared at by the few Germans we encountered, it wasn't long before we wheeled into a part of the naval premises. In the permanent brick-built barrack to which we were taken it was warm and, by Milag standards, relatively cosy. And without the necessity of going out-of-doors for *appels* and to lavatories in the severe weather, we realized that, whatever the interrogation process might hold for us, we had gained something in the basic creature comforts of dryness and warmth. Furthermore, we could look out of our upstairs window on to a church and other buildings in the street and across a small parade ground. One place frequented by civilians bore the notice 'ERNÄHRUNGSAMPT' which we translated as 'food rationing office'.

Another sight, which prompted conflicting emotions, was the burnt-out shell of a largish building that looked very much like the one we were in. One of the guards confided that it had burnt down in an air-raid because someone had failed to connect the fire hydrant to the appropriate water supply and the omission was discovered only in the emergency. One could see the unhappy hydrant standing inside the main doorway. So, the vaunted German efficiency was not infallible – a pleasant thought!

In the event of an air-raid alarm, we were told, guards would conduct us to the basement. Luckily our friends in the R.A.F. didn't test our nerves.

The food was the same old stuff and as mean in quantity. There was, however, an issue of a few German cigarettes which soothed my smoking companions in the long empty hours.

We hadn't been there long before an N.C.O. approached me to do something for him. He seemed a pleasant enough fellow, the antithesis of Herr Rompa in build and manner. All he wanted me to do was to copy in water colours a printed picture of a little German township. I never discovered why he picked on me; anyway, I was quite ready to oblige him and gain a pleasant occupation for myself instead of suffering days of boring inaction.

When the examination began we were taken one at a time, and were not returned to the room with those still to be questioned. So each of us faced the inquisitor with some apprehension. I found it difficult to imagine what information simple seamen might have that would be of use to the enemy after we had been in their custody for six months. None of us memorized codes, and knowledge of big-ship movements like the presence of MAURETANIA, QUEEN MARY and QUEEN ELIZABETH all seen in Sydney harbour together, could be flatly denied. My anxiety was centred on entirely different matters. Having been driven ashore by the depression in shipping after getting my Second Mate's 'ticket', I spent seven years immediately prior to the war in the gas industry. My speciality was the use of gas in industrial processes. For example, two of my last jobs before joining AUSTRALIND were on furnaces for hardening the noses of 20-inch projectiles in a large ammunition factory, and on building inert gas generators essential for a new plant for manufacturing aluminium powder, the principal ingredient of incendiary bombs. So, I figured I had got to hide completely the whole of this phase of my life else I might be detained here indefinitely. Certainly I had to be prepared to bridge this gap; I decided how I would do it, if necessary, and worked the idea out a bit at leisure.

At last I was summoned and conducted to a nicely furnished office. Sitting at a desk was a fine-looking, elderly naval officer with an aristocratic bearing. The orderly retired and I was politely asked to sit down in a comfortable upholstered chair. 'Please help yourself to a cigarette, Mr. Bird,' he said in a pleasant and cultivated English voice. 'I would just like to have a little chat with you.' I thanked him and declined the cigarette. Then, as I had been warned, followed a series of seemingly innocuous questions about my parentage, schooling and seafaring career, all duly noted down. 'When you completed your apprenticeship and passed your Second Mate's exam in 1931, did you continue with your company, Houlder Bros., and get your First Mate's and your Master's Certificates?'

This is where the romancing starts, I thought. He will guess there's something unusual about a man of 32 being only a Third Mate on a cargo boat in wartime. So I explained quite truthfully that after sailing before the mast for a couple of years the depression in the shipping industry forced me ashore, and then, untruthfully, I said I had joined my father on his (fictitious) farm in Rutland until the outbreak of the war. This initial fabrication tripped glibly off my lips and was noted; I couldn't go back on it now. 'That's interesting,' he said, 'farming and seafaring often go hand in hand. How big is your father's farm?' I had anticipated this, so without hesitation I said, 'It is rather small, just 75 acres.' 'Is it a dairy farm?' 'No, Sir, it is mixed, arable and pasture with cattle.' Thinking quickly I said, 'normally about 80 bullocks, and a few milkers and sheep.' The old fellow seemed to know quite a lot about farming because he retorted, 'That's rather a lot of animals on a mixed farm of that size, isn't it?' Now, I thought, we are on the unrehearsed part of the act. I had never regarded myself as quick-witted, but now, put to the test, I flashed back, 'That may seem so, Sir, but near my home the River Welland runs through rich watermeadows which, in season, are rented out for grazing, and local farmers with limited pasture can fatten their stock there.' He seemed quite interested in this idea and made a note of it; then abruptly asked, 'Do you know London? You said you sat for your examination there.' 'Yes Sir, a little.' 'It is a very interesting place,' he said. 'Have you ever gone into the history of the City?' As a matter of fact, when hanging about unemployed trying to find a ship, I had taken a keen interest in it and spent many hours reading in the Guildhall Library. So, not knowing where he was leading, I said cautiously, 'I agree with you, Sir, it is an interesting place, I of course know a little of its long history.' 'Have you ever heard of the Steelyard and do you know where it was?' 'Yes, Sir, I believe it was on the Thames near the present Cannon Street Station.' This answer seemed to please him and he said, 'You are quite right. No doubt you have heard of the Hanse Merchants who lived there.' 'Yes, Sir,' I replied. That apparently was his cue, for he then delivered a most interesting little lecture on the German Merchants resident at the 'Stilehof' from the twelfth century until they were compelled to quit in 1598. He obviously knew the history of the City intimately, and he seemed pleased that he had an appreciative audience. Again he suddenly changed course. 'Do you know the house flag of the Ellerman Shipping Company?' he asked. 'Yes, Sir,' I said, and described it. 'That's correct, and I suppose you know what the three letters J.R.E. on the flag mean?' 'Yes, Sir, they stand for J. R. Ellerman, the shipowner.' 'Mr. Bird,' he said 'you are sadly mistaken, J.R.E. means Jews Rule England.' And at that he launched into a vituperative diatribe on the Jews in general, and worked himself up to a near frenzy. It was sad to hear this cultivated old gentleman vomiting out all the crude anti-semitic propaganda of the Nazi Party. When he had exhausted himself, and, I sensed, felt a little ashamed of his uninhibited outburst, he asked, 'What do you think of the Jews in your country?' 'Well, Sir, I have met some Jews I didn't like, but (thinking of splendid Alf Ehlers, the refugee potter for whom I built a kiln) I have known others who were very fine citizens.' He didn't seem pleased with my reaction but, apparently he had shot his bolt, for he concluded the interview saying, 'Take this book and read it and think about it when you get back to your camp.' While I thanked him for it he pressed a button and a guard came in and took me to a room where the 'processed' men were kicking their heels. The book was entitled **The Eighth Crusade** and it turned out to be just another boorish exposition of the Nazi philosophy on Judaism.

On 17th February, 1942, the whole party made the return journey to Milag without notable incident. Strange to say, there was a cosy feeling of relief about getting back to the camp, the familiar barracks, rooms, friends and even the old routine. It was the little world we knew.

CHAPTER SEVEN

The Melting Pot

It was in the early and frigid weeks of 1942 that the final groups of prisoners were transferred to Milag from Sandbostel. With little else to cheer us, it was a pleasure for some to be reunited with old friends. It was a very warm occasion for my shipmate, Jim Morgan, when his brother Bill arrived.

At this time we had to queue at the galley to receive our midday dole of soup. In order to keep in the lee of the building, for the wind had a keen edge, the queue was formed in an elongated U, so as we slowly moved along, one saw and spoke to many of the other 'customers' face to face. 'I think I know you,' said one man to me, and I who had been staring hard at this strangely garbed fellow said, 'I was thinking just the same about you.' He was Harry Harper, Second Mate of KANTARA who was an A.B. on my first ship fifteen years before and now destined to play an important role in my life as a prisoner. I met three other old shipmates later.

Father Ernest (Padre Ball to us), our Anglican priest, recalls answering a summons to Feldwebel Rompa's office soon after he arrived in Sandbostel. With the feldwebel was a British Army chaplain whom at first he did not recognize. 'Then to my astonishment and delight,' he said, 'he was revealed as Geoffrey White who had been a student at Kelham (then the principal house of their Order) while I was there.' Later, Padre White succeeded Padre Ball, as Milag's Anglican chaplain.

Out of the medley of nationalities that made up our population, men who were citizens of countries occupied by the Germans were eventually singled out for repatriation. The first of my friends to go were the Dutchmen of KOTA NOPAN.

It will help some later parts of this story to fall into place if I digress and mention that, while serving my apprenticeship, I came under the influence of an unusual and interesting Quartermaster, a Swede named Alf Martin, and since then I had been fated to associate with Scandinavians. That association had generated in me a high regard for the Nordic people, so it was with pleasure that I found two Norwegians were drafted to my room, in spite of the fact that they brought the total of inmates up to eighteen.

Einar Naess, the stocky, red-haired Third Engineer of SILVAPLANA soon became a friend of mine. It was interesting to see how quickly the Norwegians established themselves in our tight little British community.

I also struck up a friendship with SILVAPLANA's First Mate, Åge Olsen, which was to have important consequences for me. This likeable and energetic young officer was a gifted linguist and he was kind enough to devote many hours a week over several months to teaching Captain Yare and myself Norwegian. Captain Yare's interest in this language arose from being trapped for months in a Norwegian port after the outbreak of war. My motive was quite different.

So far as one indulged in sentiment in Milag, I felt sorry to be parted from them, when they were repatriated.

They were scarcely out of the camp when, on 6th April, a large batch of prisoners arrived and were held incommunicado in Barrack 24, which was wired off from the rest of the camp and guarded. There was much speculation as to who they were. Gradually the truth leaked out. Ten Norwegian-owned ships had been bottled up in the neutral port of Gothenburg. Sir George Binney, who had earlier arranged the sailing of six ships that got to Britain safely, had organized a second convoy. There were British as well as Norwegian Masters aboard each ship; the majority of the crews were Norwegian. Many other Norwegians had fled their homeland and were anxious to go to Britain to take up arms against the common enemy. This second attempt to run the gauntlet was ill-starred. Two ships did get across and two returned to Gothenburg, but six had to scuttle themselves, with their valuable cargoes of ball bearings and special steel, in order to prevent the Germans taking possession of them. Their crews were picked up and taken into captivity. Of the total of 204 prisoners, 147 were Norwegian, 54 British, two were Dutch and one a Pole. Much to our excitement, there were also six women and one small girl among the captives; they were housed in what was the German Guard Room opposite the main gate and so plainly visible to us. It was not until mid-June, after they had all been interrogated, that, co-incidental with a German Admiral's visit, the barbed wire was taken down and the men were free to mingle with the rest of us. There were many fine young men amongst them, tall, dignified and well dressed in civilian clothes; unmistakably Norwegian. Three days later, when some of them were in the Camp Theatre, enjoying the current production: 'Spotlights of London', the guards suddenly descended on them, ordered them back into Barrack 24 and wired them in. There was no apparent reason for this action, nor was there for their release on 10th July, 1942. These seemingly arbitrary acts of our captors brought home to us the fact that our destiny was in their hands. Men were plunged into depression, or they cursed or burst out laughing, according to temperament and circumstances. I was an early visitor to the Norwegians' barrack to find out if there were any I knew or who had news of particular friends for me. It was clear that conditions in Norway were pretty bleak.

Many of these young men soon began to play their part in camp life, in choir, theatre and educational activities. Among them were two with whom I became especially friendly, namely, Bjørn Egge who took Olsen's place as language tutor, and a middle-aged Radio Operator, Otto Brunes. Otto was an inventive man, given to discussing all sorts of technical matters of mutual interest as we walked around our cage. Bjørn was a young man of fine presence and charming character. Like the rest of them, he was an ardent patriot burning to play an effective part in ejecting the Germans from his beloved country.

If nothing else, Milag offered one a very wide choice of friends; exclusively male, of course. The range spanned a couple of dozen nationalities, age groups from 17 to 76, talents running through most of the arts, crafts, literature and sciences; and there was a diversity of temperaments, education, religion and culture. He would be hard to please who could not find congenial company. The one thing that was lacking was the obverse of companionship – solitude.

Once accustomed to the drab surroundings, a murmuring belly and cold feet, inured to being enclosed within barbed wire, and habituated to the inane routine of *appels*, anyone so minded could lead a busy and purposeful life. Most prisoners did respond in a positive way to the challenge, though, said to relate, some unhappy souls seemed to turn in on themselves and lapse into a state of melancholic vegetation. This happened to one of my room-mates, and he ultimately went mad. For the more resilient and vigorous ones there was plenty of scope for what energies the meagre diet allowed them.

Men not classified as officers could be called upon legitimately by our captors to work outside the camp as well as inside. The number compelled to work outside was comparatively small, due, most likely, to our rural location. Most of those who worked on local farms on a regular basis, did so by choice. This was undoubtedly good for their health and morale; it was also of considerable benefit to the camp in general, as will become plain later.

Officers could not be compelled to work outside the camp, so none of them could enjoy the benefits of farm work with a clear conscience. Two officers who chose to work on farms had to endure the odium of 'working for the bloody Germans'.

In addition to the work of the Camp Captain and Barrack Captains already mentioned, there were various jobs in the camp office and the Officers' and Ratings' Welfare Committees which formed channels of communication within what one could loosely call the internal administration.

The bitterly cold weather persisted throughout March and there was still a dearth of food parcels. The larder was empty. Everywhere men thought, talked and dreamed about food and lack of smokes ad nauseam. The camp was down to the basic rations provided by the Germans. These were little enough[1].

Friends tended to get together in pairs or groups to pool rations. It was sometimes more economical and in better days sharing allowed more variety. Some 'combines' recklessly ate all their rations at one sitting. Others eked them out through the day. John Andrew, my combine mate, and I husbanded our resources. For breakfast we had two thin slices of bread with a scraping of margarine and jam, swilled down with a mug of *ersatz* coffee. For tea we had exactly the same, except that we drank what was variously described as 'mint

---

[1] *See Appendix I.*

tea', 'raspberry leaf tea' or just plain 'cat's piss'. One slice of bread we had with the main meal of the day which was half a litre of soup per man plus any cabbage, swedes or potatoes that were going. This had to be collected from the galley.

The main galley, in Barrack 12, was manned by about sixteen prisoners, half of them 'spud barbers'. Germans kept an eye on their activities. The menus did not demand the higher culinary skills that Harry Saunders, the head cook, and his staff had been accustomed to exercise on the liner ORAMA. Theirs was a rather thankless task but they made the best of the mean quantity and poor quality ingredients issued to us, and I doubt if they ever took to heart the snide allegation that in lean times the galley staff didn't lose as much weight as the rest of us.

If any good can be said to result from semi-starvation, it is probably the humbling of a man's ego. It compels him to acknowledge his dependence upon other people. For us those other people were the British Red Cross Society and Order of St. John of Jerusalem[1]. Without the Merchant Seaman's habitual attitude to life, his spirit, ingenuity and good humour, Milag would have been a poor place. But it was the Red Cross that underpinned our existence. They provided the means to maintain bodily health, and to develop the mind through books, music, arts and sport. Above all, they enabled us to keep in touch with loved ones and friends at home. The Red Cross aimed at delivering one food parcel per week to each prisoner, but in our first bad winter we had some long spells – up to six weeks – without any. As time went on, such interruptions were less frequent and of shorter duration.

Prisoners' next of kin at home were informed by the Red Cross Society that the contents of the parcels were carefully chosen to supplement German rations so as to provide a balanced diet and an interesting variety. Each parcel weighed 10lb and cost approximately 10 shillings (50p), but prisoners received them whether relatives subscribed or not[2].

---

[1] *For brevity we tended to say 'Red Cross' without distinguishing between the International Organisation at Geneva and the British Society; and we used the term to embrace the Order of St. John of Jerusalem as well.*

[2] *See Appendix II*

Sometimes the parcels we received came from the Canadian Red Cross[1]. They made a nice change. Their contents were more standardized and they had fewer but larger items. They were also of very high quality. Their large biscuits, chocolate, Spam and KLIM (powdered milk) were especially appreciated. The comparatively large KLIM tins were invaluable as cooking utensils and for the making of a variety of things. Some food of excellent quality also reached us from the generous British Community in the Argentine.

When the supply of Red Cross parcels became more constant, there was greater scope for varying the messing arrangements, especially after the provision of a couple of small galleys where the Red Cross food could be heated or cooked. When the main galley let us have boiled potatoes separate from the soup, a whole world of hash, shepherd's pie and fish rissoles was opened up.

A good deal of culinary ingenuity went into making cakes and puddings out of crushed biscuits and raisins; Canadian KLIM tins were handy utensils in which to bake them – sometimes in the ash pit of the room's bogey. The little cookhouse north of the hospital was affectionately known as 'Alec's Galley'. Alec, an Australian, presided over the officers' Red Cross galley and was soon as highly regarded for his agreeable nature as for his skill as a cook.

In some instances all the occupants of a room would form a mess combine and work out a weekly rota of duties for each man. On a grander scale, Harry Garner, an officer of great organizing ability and indefatigable energy, who did much good work for us in the camp, organized and managed an ambitious mess for officers. Participants contributed all the 'meaty' contents of their parcels and their German rations, and with the aid of Harry Saunders and his assistants, were provided with hot meals.

---

[1] *See Appendix III.*

Chapter Eight

Anatomy of Milag

It is no wonder that Red Cross parcels evoked in us emotional responses as strong as long-awaited letters from loved ones at home, or news of an Allied Victory that promised to shorten our captivity. We were in fear when the store became depleted, elated when there was a renewal of deliveries; and always thankful to receive this life-preserving bounty. The delivery of Red Cross parcels to camps throughout Germany was a great humanitarian enterprise and a remarkable feat of organization.

The work of receiving, storing, opening and distributing the parcels was a considerable undertaking. It demanded, and got, the services of men of complete integrity and administrative ability. At times it also required patience, firmness and tact in dealing with the Germans. Captain Christopher Yare, Mr. L. P. Lockie (a civilian captured as a passenger), Captain Bradley, Radio Officer Willie Russell and a junior officer or two carried out this vital service impeccably.

A large part of Barrack 9, just inside the gate, was set apart as the Parcels Office and Store, and in it the staff worked under the strict scrutiny of three Germans. Parcels were issued in barrack-by-barrack order. Men were advised by the Barrack Captain when it was their turn to collect them and each man received a parcel on presentation of his numbered *Kriegsgefangener* tally. Every parcel had to be undone and every can and packet opened or pierced to render the items unsaleable or unfit for use as bribes to the guards or native populace, and to prevent would-be escapers accumulating a stock of sustaining foodstuffs. The result was that most of the food had to be eaten within a few days of receipt. Whilst this practice was not ideal, even for those with no intention of using the food illegally, it was far better than the system at Sandbostel. There the Germans not only compelled the parcel gang to open all tins, but insisted that, regardless of their contents, they should be emptied into a bowl brought by the parcel's recipient. Sardines, milk, corned beef, jam, vegetables and rice pudding, etc., were all dumped in the bowl together. This deliberate waste provoked a near riot, and was stopped after a visit by representatives of the Red Cross.

At first, small hand openers were used, causing blistered hands and intolerable delays. The German solution to the problem was typical of the military mind. The recipient of a parcel had to lay out its contents, whereupon a guard stuck his bayonet into each innocent tin! It was not until a prisoner invented a tool – a forerunner of the openers seen nowadays clamped on kitchen walls – which opened all sorts of cans quickly and easily, that a reasonable routine was established.

Although I saw *das krankenhaus* through the window of my room in Barrack 15 every day, I had little personal experience of the camp hospital's activities. A cracked rib lashed up with sticking plaster and minor dentistry were, thankfully, the extent of my demand on its services.

One had distinct impressions of good work being done behind its doors, and one sensed that the mere existence of this place of caring and healing gave comfort to the sick and the few who actually died there.

It started humbly enough for Dr. Sperber, who achieved a great deal without much equipment. For example, he recruited a group of blood donors and, lacking any means of storing blood, gave transfusions direct from donor to patient. Percy Rossiter of ORAMA was one of the group and he told me of two such direct transfusions. One was to his shipmate, Harry Walker, who was in plaster with T.B. of the spine and had to be built up sufficiently to endure the journey to another place. In the other case a transfusion saved a young Welshman who had become so depressed that he cut his wrist in an attempt to take his own life.

The Germans seemed hostile to Dr. Sperber and gave him little or no co-operation, perhaps because he was a Czech who had got out of his country when the Nazis occupied it and had joined a British merchant ship. He was highly esteemed by the prisoners, so we were dismayed to hear that he was being whisked off to an unknown destination at very short notice. I still possess a dictionary he gave

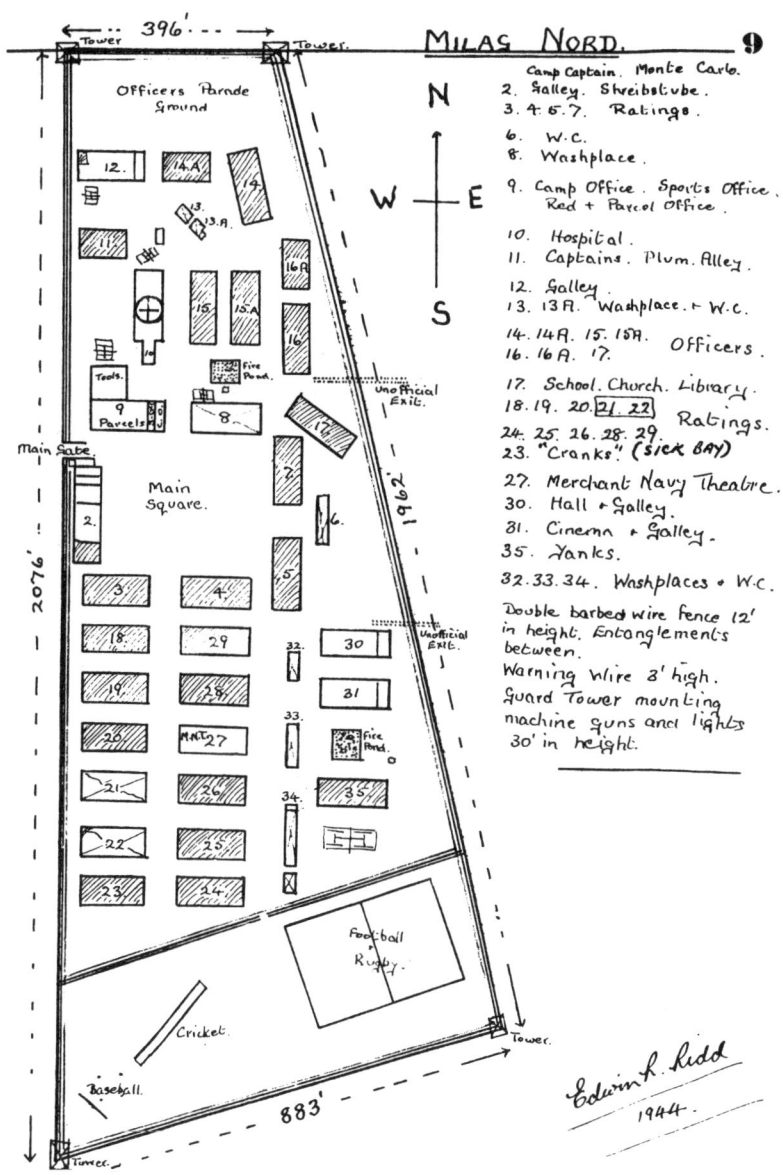

Plan of Milag Nord

me in which I recorded 'Kindly presented to me by Dr. Sperber on his departure from Milag on this foggy morning 3rd November, 1942'. When I met him by chance in London in 1945 I learned that he had been sent to a concentration camp.

His successor, Major Harvey, R.A.M.C., a first-class surgeon, came from somewhere 'outside'. Whether he carried greater authority or was more acceptable to the Germans I do not know, but he got improvements under way, and with the indispensable help of the Red Cross, built up a good hospital service for our community of nearly 3,000 men.

Captain (Toothy) Green, also from an Army P.O.W. Camp, joined him as camp dentist. Padre Ball once wondered how the several German soldiers who came to Captain Green on the quiet for treatment, would have reacted if they had found out that he was a Jew! Major Harvey saved the lives of two men, to my knowledge, by standing firm against the heavy German pressure to remove them from Milag. They were Norwegians from the Gothenburg ships and his insistence on medical grounds that they must remain under his care probably prevented their suffering the fate of many of their comrades.

The Germans treated harshly nationals of occupied countries who, in their view, had no right to prisoner-of-war status. They behaved more reasonably to us.

When Chief Officer Henderson of S.S. DEVON developed an uncommon disease of the liver, presumably contracted out East, and wasted away to skin and bone, he was taken to a hospital for tropical diseases in Hamburg. He was away for so many weeks that we feared for his life. Suddenly he returned looking plump and healthy, a new man, and so he remained.

From the beginning there were men intent on serving those of their fellow prisoners who wanted to express their religious sentiments in a formal way or felt the need of spiritual support. I had been brought up in the Anglican Church, but going to sea at the age of sixteen effectively broke my church-going habit; like most adolescents, I entertained doubts of the truth and validity of the orthodox tenets and eventually became an agnostic. But in Milag I attended services and joined the Anglican choir because I enjoyed singing. It was satisfying, too, to use certain practical talents I possessed in the service of the church.

Accidents of war had brought together in Milag a number of priests of various persuasions who performed their offices in as nearly normal a way as circumstances permitted. Padre Ball, more accurately Father Ernest of the Society of the Sacred Mission, was an Anglican monk. He, too, had had an adventurous round-the-world journey to Milag. In August, 1940,he had sailed as one of the escorts for children being evacuated from Britain to relatives in Australia, via Cape Town. On completing this task he was given a passage home via New Zealand. A pair of raiders intercepted and sank the liner RANGITANE on which he was a passenger and, after transfer to two other ships in turn, he completed the circumnavigation by way of Cape Horn and was landed at Bordeaux.

A Salvation Army Officer, Brigadier Best, had sailed to Australia, also as an escort, in the same ship as Padre Ball. The vessel in which he sailed for home took a different route from RANGITANE but suffered the same fate. Captured by another raider, eventually he was reunited with Padre Ball in Milag Nord.

These two held undenominational services in the main hall every Sunday morning which were well attended and greatly appreciated.

Padre Ball was allotted a room in Barrack 17 for use as an Anglican chapel, and he recruited the appropriate skills to furnish and adorn it to make it a quiet place apart from the hurly-burly of camp life. A carpenter made a cross and candlesticks; Frank Vicovari embroidered a frontal for the table serving as an altar; and Stan Hugill painted a picture of 'The Risen Christ' to hang behind the altar. When the materials became available I used artists' oil paints to simulate designs in stained glass on the windows, and painted a Nativity picture for use on the altar at Christmas. This chapel was used mainly for evensong and the celebration of Holy Communion.

Adherents of the Roman Catholic Church were very well served with clergy. No fewer than ten French Canadian priests and five Lay Brothers, on their way to a mission station in Basutoland, had been captured together on ZAM ZAM. They too had a room in Barrack 17, which also was lovingly transformed into a chapel. Again, willing hands, not all of them Roman Catholic, applied their skills to the task. Tom Burke, a Second Mate, painted two pictures for the altar, 'Stella Maris' and 'The Agony in the Garden', and fourteen smaller ones of the Stations of the Cross. A Sanctuary Lamp was carved by 'Chippy' Frensham and a large peg rug style carpet was made by the Chief Hospital Orderly, aided by patients enjoying occupational therapy. This remarkable carpet depicted St. George and the Dragon. After the war the contents of the R.C. Chapel were taken to Africa and put in a small Mission Chapel there, and dedicated to Prisoners of War.

Besides the admirable Parcels Gang, Galley Staff, Barbers and those called upon to do the less salubrious chores, others devoted their time to the continual work of the Post Office and the more fitful issuing of clothing and boots.

The Post Office required men capable of performing methodically and unfailingly the routine distribution of blank letter forms and cards to the barracks, and the more congenial task of taking round letters from home. The handling of private parcels, after the German censors had gone through them, demanded the utmost honesty.

In the early months, the allocation and issuing of the totally inadequate supply of clothing and boots, both ex-German and British Army stuff received through the Red Cross, was a most important yet thankless task, for there were so many ill-clad men in the prevailing bad weather. Captain Carr of R.M.S. NATIA, exercising the judgment of Solomon, fulfilled the role with scrupulous impartiality which was not always appreciated by those whose hopes for and real need of, say, an army great coat, were disappointed.

With so many men selflessly serving the camp in their various ways, I did not hesitate to accept an invitation to do a job for the common weal.

A problem that needed urgent attention was the bad condition of much of the footwear, and my brief was to help organize and administer a boot and clothes repair service to improve that situation. The memory of my own misery in wet, cold feet was, no doubt, another incentive to get on with this particular job. As it turned out, this occupation was to be of use to me in the future, in a way undreamt of when I took it on.

There were a few competent cobblers and tailors working for the camp. But the Germans supplied them only scrap material to work with, and their efforts were not properly directed in the general interest of the inmates. The first move was to consult them and set a daily target of repairs.

There were so many men in distress that it was very difficult to decide who should be put at the head of the queue. This was settled by rationing each barrack to five pairs of boots and three articles of clothing a week, and the Barrack Captains had the unenviable task of nominating men to hand in work on the Repair Day allotted to each barrack. This arrangement was another severe test of wisdom and integrity of the Barrack Captains.

The Bootery, as we called our centre of operations (actually a corner of the First Station next to the Parcel Office), was open at stated times each week day for the receipt of properly labelled articles, which were carefully recorded. Losses had been an unhappy feature of the previous 'free for all' arrangement.

The cobblers and tailors, who did the work outside Milag, at Lager 3, under German supervision, collected the day's quota when they returned to the camp for *Mittagessen*. The completed repairs would be returned next midday, ready for their owners to collect.

The cobblers were handicapped by the poor quality of materials and the dilapidated state of the boots, and in a few months it was found we were hardly stemming the tide. The tailors, however, managed to cope with the clothes repairs. Fortunately, about this time we received a supply of good leather through the Red Cross, so more cobblers were trained and the total output of work doubled, and soon afterwards the tide turned. To make their rather monotonous job a little more congenial, the Germans were persuaded to excuse them from attending the irksome midday *appel*; and a payment to them from Camp Funds was made, in addition to the twelve Reichmarks a month which each man received from the Germans. By the end of the first year operation, 5,045 pairs of boots and 668 garments had been repaired. More significant was the fact that the rate of boot repairs was now enough to maintain the camp's footwear in reasonable condition.

Apart from the satisfaction of doing a bit for one's campmates, there were a few bright spots in the routine. I shall never forget one thrilling incident. It may not seem very thrilling to handle a heap of dilapidated boots. But these boots, which had come from the Interrogation Lager, were very special boots with unusual soles; they were British Commando boots just off the feet of real fighting men of the British Forces, who had landed and fought on the docks at St. Nazaire a few days earlier.

Shortly we were to see their owners, wounded men swathed in bandages, their clothing tattered, proceeding in a group to the German dressing station up the road. Despite their wounds, they marched with vigour and precision AT THE DOUBLE, taunting the German guards to keep up with them as they went. A brave sight! It was a wonderful tonic for us.

Another service, which had more colourful overtones and shadier undertones than the staid bootery, was the Canteen. This was really a 'service' provided by the German Authorities for the prisoners' benefit. Actually, in the British Forces' concept of a canteen, ours was a bit of a joke.

For convenience it had two 'shops', one for ratings located in the hall on the *platz* and one for officers in the little hut just to the north of Barrack 15. Mr. Hunter was in charge of the former and John Watson presided over the latter and had general responsibility for the whole business. The shops opened at stated times in mid-morning and mid-afternoon on weekdays. Unfortunately, they hadn't much to sell! Toilet paper in large coarse grey sheets was usually available, so were pencils with splintery wood and poor leads; they were the only means of writing allowed. It was oddly satisfying to make a purchase when one had been denied this commonplace pleasure for many months. Occasionally, slightly better note-books were to be had; and poor razor blades, toothbrushes of sorts, and cigarette papers were on sale. There was sometimes an aerated drink available called 'Brauser' which Watson advertised rather aptly as being 'rich in vitamin P'. I never heard of anyone becoming hooked on it!

All of these items were obtained through the German Quartermaster's Stores against payment, and accurate account was kept of sales and stock. Any profit was credited to our hospital. The German Quartermaster, Korveten Kapitän Müller, inspected the books at frequent intervals to ensure that Watson & Co. hadn't played fast and loose with the precious goods entrusted to their care. The gallant captain took the opportunity of his periodic visits to collect his tribute of 'Craven Mixture', a pipe tobacco that by insidious suggestion he had come to believe was the most highly prized smoke in Britain, and he gradually became addicted to it and wanted no other brand. The taste of pipe smokers in the camp was, in fact, quite different, so in 'good times' this brand was comparatively cheap, abundant and easy for Watson to acquire.

Now John Watson was a very presentable member of our community and Kapitän Müller and his Quartermaster Sergeants discovered that he was also diplomatic and discreet. In consequence they came to trust him and before long the Sergeants (one of whom was a Lion Tamer in peacetime) found in him an admirable partner for furthering their own private business aspirations.

Sale of goods or barter between Germans and prisoners was strictly forbidden, except officially through the canteen, and if any illegal transaction involved the misappropriation of German military stores the consequences of detection would undoubtedly have been dire. It was therefore necessary to keep the machinery of this business well oiled so that it ran smoothly and silently.

As already hinted, a significant factor in our relationship with our captors was that they, with a few exceptions, had very easy consciences about accepting bribes. Of course, we paupers had no fund of Reichmarks to draw upon, but when parcels were getting through from home we had one commodity more highly prized than money, namely *Englishcher Zigaretten* and *Tobak*. So bribes, tacitly approved by our own 'top brass', were discreetly dispensed regularly, even to the Second in Command and a couple of key men down the line, so as to ensure that the real rogues, the Quartermaster Sergeants, could carry on their business with Watson and Harry Saunders of the galley, with relative impunity.

Naturally, this risky business was kept a close secret on both sides of the wire. I only got the merest peep of the tip of the tip of this iceberg of corruption through my friend Captain Carr, who was close to our Camp Captain.

The deals that Watson & Co., made were done on a wholesale scale, as compared with the petty hole-in-corner exchanges with the guards that we ordinary prisoners indulged in. They would buy sacks of flour, for example, not a couple of eggs and an onion.

The story that I like best has a nice streak of wry humour in it. Matches were usually scarce and at one time they were so scarce that even the German camp was short of them. It so happened that, preceding this dearth, parcels had been arriving fairly freely, so Watson and his backers had laid up a good stock of the wherewithal against future opportunities. When a consignment of matches arrived to relieve the situation for the Germans, Watson was able to buy the lion's share of them. The happy outcome was that he was able to sell a lot of them, 'under the counter' to needy German guards who paid an inflated price in Reichmarks.

Through the friendship John had established with the Quartermasters he was able to obtain many things of value for us, and some unusual ones like silk stockings for our 'actresses', the loan of ropes for boxing rings, and even hire of theatrical costumes.

A nice feature of this trade was that the Germans delivered the goods into the camp, under guard and right into the Canteen's locked storeroom.

When the illegal goods were sold, the transactions were also meticulously accounted for, but in another book which Kapitän Müller was not privileged to inspect. The considerable profit was also given to the hospital. With these funds Major Harvey obtained additional drugs and extra equipment. I can't say what 'palm oiling' he had to do to achieve his ends!

In all this risky business Watson never fell foul of the Authorities. It was therefore ironic that he got into serious trouble, quite unwittingly, in the course of perfectly legitimate trading. The Germans had made available for sale in the canteen a barrel of pickled mixed vegetables. As they were not particularly appealing to the eye or palate and were not selling well, for it was not a time of famine, Watson had to resort to advertising. With the licence of an ad-man he described the tart concoction as 'Russian Salad'. The Germans were not familiar with this appellation and, as they had just suffered great loss and humiliation on the Eastern Front, they took it amiss and threatened Watson with transportation to a camp of correction to revise his sense of humour. He escaped that fate only after the Germans had accepted a sworn statement from the chefs of ORAMA that it was in fact the correct description of the stuff in English.

A customer at the canteen would sometimes notice the somewhat pretentious wording in fine gothic script stamped on paperware, *In der kantine des Marlag und Milag gekauft* (purchased in the canteen at Marlag and Milag Nord). Payment was made in Lager Gold (camp money) specially printed by the German Authorities for use only in P.O.W. camps and issued in notes of 1, 10 and 50 pfennig, and 1, 2, 5 and 10 Reichmark denominations. Each prisoner received 10 R.M. a month and an equivalent amount, i.e. £1, was deducted from his pay at home. The international financial transaction involved in getting this money to us was carried out through the Protecting Power, Switzerland, and we consequently knew it as 'Embassy Money'. There was little enough to spend it on. Optimists could bank it, but I suppose its greatest use was for gambling.

The real medium of exchange was the cigarette, though packets of tea sometimes served that purpose. Barter flourished within the camp because some naturally preferred meat to fish, biscuits to chocolate, etc., and when the Indians were brought into the camp some of them would not eat meat on religious grounds and wanted fish and vegetables. However, when it came to comparing the value of one commodity with another, that would most likely be done in terms of cigarettes. And as we became more sophisticated in trading, differences in barter values would be adjusted by payment in cigarettes. As in the real world, the value of our 'currency' fluctuated. A prolonged hiatus in the receipt of Red Cross parcels or mail, would send the value bounding upward, just as a steady inflow would stabilize or depress it. When more prosperous times were upon the camp and men had some reserves, a trading class evolved which made it its business to acquire goods and sell them for a profit. Such operators had to watch the 'money market' closely to avoid loss due to unfavourable exchange rates. They served a useful purpose and no doubt got some satisfaction out of it themselves.

It was the cigarette that enabled us to procure eggs, vegetables and occasionally, even poultry from 'outside', generally by way of the 'farmers' or others on working parties. This business was, of course, *verboten*, but there were, besides bribery, many ways of outwitting the guards who searched prisoners going out and coming in the gate. There was also some trade done with guards whose duties brought them into the camp. Through this channel illegal articles like knives and certain tools were procured.

But this trade had its dangerous side.

Not long after 'lights out', perhaps it was eleven o'clock on Friday, 15th May, 1942, a rifle shot rang out nearby which got us out of bunks instantly. At first, in the darkness, nothing could be seen from our window; then, after waiting apprehensively for a long while, we discerned the dark shapes of a stretcher party carrying a body into the hospital opposite.

Full of foreboding, we could hardly sleep that night.

Next day we heard what had happened.

A likeable young Radio Officer, Walter Skett, living in Barrack 16, had arranged to do a small barter with a guard who was listed to patrol inside the camp that night. For that purpose he had – quite improperly – gone outside, somewhere to the north of his barrack, to keep the appointment. By the irony of fate the friendly guard had been replaced by another who knew nothing of the intended business and when approached, it was said, did not get the proper response to his challenge, so opened fire with his rifle. The shot felled Walter and he soon died from the wound.

The gloomy shadow of this incident rested upon us for many a day after we had buried him in the new cemetery near the camp.

For survival and retention of sanity it would seem, on balance, the human being must put an optimistic interpretation on his predicament. And that seemed to be confirmed by the reaction of most men individually and in their corporate activities in Milag. However, gloom and depression were also part of our lot. It might affect us corporately, as just described, or it might be deeply personal such as the loss of a loved one by enemy action at home. Just three months after the shooting of Walter Skett another tragedy saddened those of us who knew and esteemed the Dutchmen of KOTA NOPAN. A letter from Captain Hatenboer, who on repatriation had enjoyed a couple of months at home with his beloved wife and family after an absence of three years, disclosed that an Allied air raid on Rotterdam's harbour had killed his wife and youngest son and destroyed his home. Still strong in his faith, he wrote, 'Indeed it is difficult to understand but "your ways are not my ways" saith the Lord.'

CHAPTER NINE

Curtain Up

Though we were powerless to influence the course of the war, we were acutely conscious that our future depended on its outcome and so we were anxious to pick up every crumb of news that we could.

Every day we were treated to Lord Haw-Haw's version of events, in English, over the Camp's loud speaker, but even the most naive *'geffie'* regarded that source with scepticism. Some fellows who were learning German would buy newspapers and get Goebbels's version of events – which was, of course, the same, except it lacked Haw-Haw's scornful tone.

Another source of news was The Camp, a newspaper for P.O.W.s in English produced by the Germans. It was supposed to be delivered weekly. Of one folded sheet, which gave it four numbered pages, it carried a number of standard features. The 'Weekly Military Survey' on the front page generally damaged credibility of the rest of the news. That was a pity, for to be fair to The Camp its 'Home News in Brief' often contained British domestic news of real interest, like plans for the post-war welfare state. But, even in this column, the Editor couldn't refrain from slipping in a barbed item, true or false, like 'A mass trial is pending in England against 1,200 miners who refused to return to work'. 'World and World News' sometimes gave us a clue as to what was going on in unexpected places, and perhaps did it unwittingly, as in an item intended to discredit Tito's guerillas: 'Following heavy losses, Tito has had to conscript women into his armed forces. A British officer reports that 15% of his band are women.' There was a 'Sports Section' giving mostly British match results. There were usually a couple of articles and verse by P.O.W.s and a Crossword Puzzle.

For my part, the stench of German propaganda vitiated The Camp and I could scarcely bring myself to read it through. But there was always the hope of gleaning an inkling of the truth by 'reading between the lines'.

The craving for news became obsessive in some men and out of it grew that most tiresome self-imposed burden – rumour-mongering. People thus afflicted might come into the room at any hour and say, 'Flash!', then come out with 'the latest', which usually was something based on wishful thinking or complete rubbish.

Our Radio Officers, still commonly called Wireless Operators, or more usually 'Sparks', whose prestige as seafarers had been greatly enhanced by their bravery under enemy attack, now set about the task of plucking the B.B.C. news out of the ether for us.

Schoolboys of an earlier generation would know that a crystal set radio receiver is comparatively easy to make, very compact, and does not require an electric current from a battery or mains to operate it. The problem in Milag was to get hold of a suitable crystal, fine lacquered copper wire and headphones.

One early source of wire was the Feldwebel's bike. He thoughtlessly brought it into the camp and left it unattended while he went about his business. Almost before his back was turned the lighting dynamo had been wrenched off, taken away and buried till the hue and cry was over.

Incredibly, someone in the camp had a crystal big enough to be divided into several smaller pieces. The jeweller who carried out this delicate process later confessed that he had held his breath lest the whole precious thing should disintegrate into powder. The first earphone was stolen from a telephone in the village and re-wound in the camp. Later ear-phones were actually made in the camp when certain soft iron bunk fittings were found to be suitable for the magnets and wire of the right sort for the coils was procured. One solution to the problem of rigging an unobtrusive aerial was the use of the metal conduit that protected the barrack's electric light wiring. This tubing was made of comparatively soft non-ferrous alloy. After disconnecting the earthing wire outside the barrack, the operator simply stuck a sail needle into it and attached a wire to the set. In an emergency it could be quickly disconnected.

Because radio sets were a prime target, and Radio Officers were high on Güsfeld's list of suspects, it was necessary to disguise the apparatus to foil the snoopers when the camp was searched. The first set was in a bakelite shaving stick case, a common enough object among our few possessions, but that was discovered during a search. Subsequently, a thermos flask, a false-bottomed tea caddy and a pocket-sized cigarette making kit with tobacco and papers atop, were tried.

The inspiration for the most ingenious disguise of the lot came in an odd way. 'Bish' Rowencroft and Eric Ackland (the librarian) were giving impersonations of the Western Brothers – who were renowned for their prominent teeth. Captain 'Toothy' Green had obliged our two comedians by making a set of big front teeth to fit over Bish's own, and a complete upper plate for Eric to substitute for his own dentures. Before their act was billed to go on, Eric sought in vain for his mislaid 'choppers'. There was a frantic search for them back stage. Happily they were found just in time for the act, and as Eric put them in his mouth a sharp-eyed and inventive Sparks who had helped in the search, saw them and had a brainwave. The result was a crystal set built into an upper denture which could be worn by its owner when on a search *appel*. Of course, he couldn't sing an operatic aria or eat sauerkraut with them in position, but that didn't matter for such activities were anyway *verboten* on *appel*. A fine point about the design was the concealment of the crystal inside a molar. When in use as a receiver the molar was pulled out and inverted, exposing the crystal for the application of the cat's whisker.

Later on, a valve set was stolen from one of the German barracks by a prisoner working there. Smuggled into Milag, it was stripped down and housed in a large book belonging to the library, the pages of which had been hollowed out to accommodate it. The connection for the detachable plug-in earphones was made of a pair of boot eyelets. The few operators were sworn to secrecy and the B.B.C. news obtained was distributed orally to each Barrack Captain who had no idea as to its exact source.

The necessarily clandestine nature of the operation was grist to the mill of the rumour-mongers; in the end the ordinary chap about the camp didn't know what to believe.

Of all the activities in Milag, beside those basic to our material and spiritual welfare, music and drama were paramount. Sports, and even gambling, were rated highly but they diverted our attention only while they lasted, whereas music and drama, at their best, elevated our spirits and took us right out of ourselves.

All such creativity within the 'wire' was the spontaneous expression of a wealth of latent talent, but it was difficult to sustain without some 'outside' assistance, and that was slow in coming. Patience and persistence were demanded.

There were two orchestras, a choir, and a goodly number of actors and performers who tended to group under one or other of the several producers; and there were individual instrumentalists and performers.

The Orama Band grew out of the ship's original orchestra of four players. When ORAMA was sunk on the ill-starred Norwegian campaign, their instruments were lost, but during a year's incarceration in Wulzburg castle, more were acquired; the band revived and a few more joined it. In the subsequent transportation to Sandbostel the players were again deprived of their instruments. After further trials of patience they were re-equipped by the British Red Cross Society about the time they moved to Marlag and Milag Nord. By degrees their number increased to twenty instrumentalists who developed into a very fine orchestra. Their repertoire tended to light classical compositions. In the early years their scope was very limited by the lack of scores and the dire shortage even of paper on which to orchestrate familiar works themselves. As time passed a good library of scores was built up, largely through the generosity of shipowners and private persons in Britain. The Orama Band was closely associated with the choir, and together they put on some excellent and memorable performances.

The other orchestra developed under the inspiration and musical talent of its namesake. The Stan Phillips Orchestra was also associated with some notable stage productions and played 'popular' music in revues and variety shows; also dance music. The problem of obtaining or writing music for this band was, of course, no easier than for the other.

The church choirs in Sandbostel were the nurseries of vocal talent, and from them sprang the choir that sang secular works. When all merchantmen were concentrated in Milag in the beginning of 1942, a group of six formed under the leadership of Mr. Sinclair, who was in possession of four pieces of music for male voices. One of the first pieces of music for male voices. One of the first pieces they learnt was 'All in the April Evening' by Sir Hugh Roberton. But there was nothing vernal about the conditions in the empty barrack in which they practised in that bitterly cold winter, and only dogged enthusiasm could have driven them to draw the musical staves and write down their parts, on scraps of wallpaper, with benumbed fingers. A piano-accordion was used to learn the different parts. Jimmy Rapp took over the direction of the choir; and he and 'Stew' Stewart invented the name Chordites by which the group became known and famous.

By the chance of war, Henry Mollison, an actor of the London stage, was captured as a passenger on a merchant ship and imprisoned with us in Milag Nord. His presence was a great boon, for he readily shared his professional skills and experience with aspiring amateurs. Furthermore, the high standard he set was a challenge and inspiration to the rest.

Even before the grim winter of 1941/42 had vented all its icy spite upon us, there were already staged praiseworthy theatrical and musical events that alleviated the depressing effect of our circumstances. And, as the months passed, producers, script-writers, actors, yes and 'actresses', emerged from all sorts of backgrounds; nor was there a lack of inventiveness, artistry and skills in respect of scenery, costumes and lighting, to support the shows.

'Robbie' Robinson, one of the back-stage crew, was an example of how sheer native talent can blossom if it has a chance. Robbie was a rating who had formerly been a docker in the Port of Liverpool – not a place famous for haute couture. In build and general appearance he was a most unlikely looking seamstress, yet Robbie could create the loveliest of feminine attire if only someone could produce a sheet, needle and cotton for him.

To give visual credibility to our 'actresses', wigs were as necessary as dress and make-up. Wig-making was not one of the nautical arts so it had to be learnt from scratch. The hair was made from the three-stranded sisal string that tied up the Red Cross food parcels. Suitable lengths were each knotted at one end and hanks of them were steeped in very hot water to soften the fibres. The strings were then attached by their knotted ends in a simple and ingenious way to a wooden batten. Hanging wet and limp, they would be combed down to straight fibres. While still on the batten the fibres would be immersed in a dye made to the requisite colour from dye-stuff which the Germans permitted us to buy from them for use in the theatre. Battens laden with the dyed yarn would then be hung up to dry.

The base of each wig was a skull cap made to measure for each 'actress'. The cap was made of fine material supplied in rolls by the Red Cross to Sikhs for making their turbans – in accordance with the Geneva Convention concerning Religious Practices – and the Sikhs donated some of it to the theatre. The 'hair' was painstakingly stitched on to the cap and the coiffure created in keeping with the stage part to be played. The cap was stuck on to the user's forehead with spirit gum and the wig was held securely in position by an elastic band.

The orchestras and the Chordites, of course, made possible productions such as The Student Prince, The Vagabond King, The Desert Song and The Mikado. These and other musical productions often brought appreciative German off-duty guards into the audience.

Major productions took about three months to prepare and stage, and between twelve and seventeen separate events were put on each year. It follows that a good many people were involved in our world of music and drama. Intervals between the weightier productions were filled with originally created revues, 'smokos', piano recitals and, later in the war, recitals of music on a gramophone.

There was one, quite unexpected, source of drama, namely the Indian crews of British ships. Several hundred Lascar crewmen had been kept imprisoned for a year or more in a separate camp several miles from Milag. They received scant consideration from their Nazi captors, and their misery was compounded by their inability to communicate with their families, or shipping companies, particularly regarding the allotment of money to their folk at home. The Germans claimed that they had no censor who understood Hindustani.

When eventually they were transferred to Milag, kindly Albert Kendal visited his own crew and discovered their plight. His solution was to hold weekly letter writing sessions. With a team of six British colleagues he would go to the Indians' barracks, where all those who wished to have letters written were assembled. Translating from Hindustani he would dictate messages in English to his scribes, moving from one client to another and checking the accuracy of his scribes. Before a message was committed to precious letter-form, he read it back to the sender in Hindustani to make sure there was no mistake. After these sessions the grateful Indians treated Albert and his colleagues to tea and real Indian chapattis.

After the war there was a nice sequel. Albert was standing by a ship undergoing repairs in Calcutta, and when it was re-commissioned he had to select a crew. At that time there was rioting around the shipping office and some ships' officers went in fear of their lives when signing on crews. Albert had no trouble, much to the astonishment of the shipping office clerks, for he had been spotted by some of his Milag friends.

It was these same friends who wished to stage a play; with interest and curiosity we filled the hall on the first night of King Akbar. Though it was not to be expected that the unfamiliar sounds of the accompanying Oriental music would flatter the western ear at the first audition, the Indians gave a fine performance to which the audience responded with delight. It established a lasting respect for the Indian theatre company and also enhanced the status of their compatriots in the camp.

Whilst the normal run of productions depended upon enthusiastic teamwork, Stan Hugill, who had a touch of the 'Treasure Island' romantic about him, distinguished himself by writing and producing two plays for which he also painted the scenery and made the costumes. He also acted in one of them.

For some, who became deeply involved in show after show, the theatre became almost the real world. *Appels*, tedious queues, petty duties, all were annoying distractions. Some 'star' performers were to be seen pacing round the camp earnestly reciting their lines, oblivious of their surroundings. Some were liable to temperamental outbursts as 'the night' approached. True to life, leading ladies were not unaffected by tantrums!

I was fortunate enough to get a glimpse of theatrical life back stage by helping John Weston, a talented artist, in the creation of stage sets, particularly the four sets required for The Desert Song. To

"PANTO PIE"

written and produced by
Arthur Gatward and Percy Williams

Act I
Scene 1. A fairy glen
   " 2. A London waterfront
   " 3. On board the "Jolly Roger"

Act II
Scene 1. Crusoe's island
   " 2. Interior of Crusoe's hut

Act III
Scene 1. Bluebeard's harem cave
   " 2. An island creek
   " 3. The fairy Queen's palace

Finale

CAST
(In order of appearance)

Genie	R. Taylor
Evil spirit	H. Mollison
Snow white } the ugly sisters	C. Mann
Goldilocks }	P. Williams
Harrietta (the fairy Queen)	H. Cousens
Dick Whittington	J. Jones
Felix (his cat)	J. Barling
Cinderella	E. Johnson
Red riding hood	P. Brady
Aladdin	M. Lewis
Boy blue	J. Green
Bo-peep	B. Brickles
Bosun	J. Bowman
Padre	R. Roswell
Drunken sailor	F. Williamson
Sindbad	S. Phillips
Seaman Brown	R. Roswell
Robinson Crusoe	N. Longmuir
Man Friday	A. Gatward
Jack } the babes	F. Williamson
Jill }	A. Jeffries
Ali Baba	J. Lawrence
Bluebeard	J. Thornton

Pirates, sailors, slaves etc.

Speciality dancers: J. Lally / T. Brown / R. Blake / R. Detain
Routines arranged by Ransford Boi / S. Bellew
The "Chordites" male voice choir, directed by J. Rapp
Music arranged by F. Goodman

Original musical numbers by F. Goodman:
"In an orange blossom garden" and "Brigands' song"

The "Orama" orchestra

F. Goodman (piano, director). N. Block (violin, leader)
Violins: L. Dell, H. Stray-Johansen, H. W. Johnson, J. Davidson
Trumpets: C. Knuckey, G. Steen-Johannessen
Trombone: A. Holmes. Cello: A. S. Hart. Clarinet: K. Andrews
Bass: J. Bolesworth. Drums: R. Mays
Hawaiian guitars:
G. Glossop, Carlos de-Paas, R. Heddle, P. O'Flynn, J. Lyons
Scenery designed and painted by S. H. Hugill

M. N. Theatre controlling body
H. Mollison (chairman). Capt. J. Thornton (Vice chairman)
P. Williams (treasurer). A. Gatward. C. Mann
H. Cousens. S. Phillips. H. Mitchinson (secretary)

M. N. Theatre permanent staff
Chief construction: Capt. Atthill, O. B. E.

Carpenters:
H. Binney, B. Pollard, J. Baker

Electricians:
W. Henning, W. Riley

Costumes and props:
W. Robinson, S. Satchell, W. Hayes, J. Lewis
J. Carpenter, G. Oxborrow

Make-up:
D. Moore, J. Mallett, W. Evans, R. Middleton, E. Acland, M. Condry

Wigs:
G. Thompson

Scenic artists:
S. J. Hugill, J. Weston, J. Cross, R. Middleton

Bookings:
R. Boswell, R. O'shea, K. Goderidge, N. Carter
Stage director: A. Caro. Stage manager: W. Garrod

Asst. stage managers:
F. Domina, R Eaddy

Stage staff:
W. Hughes, J Lewis, S. Crucis, L. Hatton, J. Matthews, O. Rayner

Posters:
A. L. Hopkin, R. Middleton

Programme designed by A. L. HOPKIN

M. N. Theatre's 1942 productions:

"Aladdin's lamp"
written and produced by
C. Mann, P. Williams, J. Lawrence and G. F. O'Bryen

"Bon voyage"
written and produced by C. Mann and G. F. O'Bryen

"Snow white and the seven twerps"
written and produced by H. Mollison

"To night's the night"
written and produced by H. Cousens

"Private lives"
produced by H. Mollison

"Spotlights of London"
written and produced by C. Mann and P. Williams

"The Vagabond King"
produced by H. Mollison

"Murder on the second floor"
adapted and produced by A. Gatward

"Brightlights"
written and produced by C. Mann and J. Rowcroft

ALSO

"Bandwagons" produced by H. Cousens
"Smokos"   „   „ H. Mollison
"Ragtime"   „   „ C. Mann
"Music hall"   „   „ H. Mollison

see a set grow out of Red Cross parcel boxes, odd bits of plywood and battens, and come to life under John's deft paintbrush strokes, was quite thrilling.

As the first night loomed, a sense of urgency, bordering on panic, built up back stage and was not dispelled until the final curtain of the dress rehearsal.

The musical romance of Harbech, Hammerstein & Mandel, with Sigmund Romberg's memorable tunes, was just the right sentimental diet for Milag at that time, and we had the actors, 'actresses' and vocal and instrumental talent under Henry Mollison's direction to do justice to it.

I shall never forget that first night. The theatre hall soon filled with ticket holders, all anticipating a great show. It was an animated scene of khaki clad figures finding their places and joking with pals on the way, for this was a 'night out'. Suddenly there was a crisp command, 'ACHTUNG!'. The idle chatter subsided abruptly and we all stood to attention as our new overlord, Kapitän Hensell (who to our relief had recently replaced 'Sauerkraut') and our Captain Notman, followed by a small German entourage, marched in and took their reserved seats in the front row.

The lights dimmed. The curtain rose gently to reveal a convincing bandit's hide-out in the soft orange-red glow of the spotlights. Powerful male voices that matched the menacing appearance of the Riffs who animated the scene sang the opening chorus. And the enigmatic figure of The Red Shadow appeared on the stage.

By the time the second refrain of The Riff Song was being sung our toes were tapping. All that followed seemed real and utterly convincing; the ladies too. Our romance-starved hearts melted.

As the curtain came down amid tumultuous applause, Kapitän Hensell jumped to his feet, turned to face the audience and with arms flung up into the air roared out – 'MILAG I'M PROUD OF YOU!'

CHAPTER TEN

Sport in Milag

When the Spring burst upon us, late but suddenly, in 1942, men of sporting instinct got the urge to hit and kick balls about, and others, ambling round the camp, longed to break into a sprint. These enthusiasms and talents of the many young men were soon channelled into a wide range of sporting activities by THE MILAG SPORTS ORGANIZATION, to the benefit of the players themselves and much to the enrichment of camp life in general. The M.S.O. was composed of competent players in various sports and others with a flair for administration; all with a zeal for getting on with the job.

The principal sports indulged in were soccer, cricket, athletics and boxing. Rugger, ice hockey, tennis and baseball also had devotees, as did indoor games such as table tennis.

It may seem incongruous that men on a low diet should wish, and were strong enough, to participate in strenuous sports, but young men of action need a physical means of self-expression and personal fulfilment, and nature has her own inbuilt regulator which dictates that output of work is proportional to the input of energy. As the majority subsisted on the same diet none had an advantage. Sometimes the doctor offered cautionary advice, particularly to boxers. Normally it was a matter of common sense.

Soccer attracted more players and fans than any other game, though cricket enthusiasts might dispute that assertion.

As conditions improved in the Spring of 1942, and equipment including footballs, was made or somehow procured (some was generously sent by the ship-owners), the first football league was formed. Eleven barracks fielded teams.

The games were played on the hard cinder/sand surface of the main *Platz* which made for fast play but offered none-too-soft landing in the event of a tumble.

The disadvantage of building the teams on a barrack basis was highlighted in that first season by Barrack 18's runaway victories –

eighteen wins from twenty matches played. Some barracks had more than their share of talent. So the M.S.O. set about grading players and composing teams which could compete with one another on a more or less equal footing, creating more interest for players and spectators alike. Two leagues, each of sixteen teams, played in the second season.

To give players a sense of identity and foster rivalry between them, teams were named after well-known British clubs. Shirts were dyed in the appropriate colours and the correct markings and emblems improvised. Later, some players received proper football kit in parcels from home.

Halfway through this season it was decreed that henceforth all football must be played on the newly-opened extension of the camp site at the bottom of 'Siberia'. This provided a fairly level pitch and the sandy soil dried quickly after rain but it did slow down the game considerably.

Five-a-side competitions were also fielded, so it wasn't long before spectators could watch at least one match a day. By degrees teams developed their own personalities and reputations, and the loyalty of fans grew around them. The enthusiasm of the spectators also became more exuberant and their vocal support from the touch-lines was often heard in the distant corners of the camp. It was on Sundays when 'international' matches were played, e.g. Scotland v. England, Thames v. Merseyside, that partisanship reached its highest pitch.

The general run of seafarers were less familiar with rugby football and much less interested. Those who had played it at school knew that the hard surface of the *Platz* would break bones or graze the hide off anyone who ventured to play this game on it.

All this changed when the new 'sports field' was opened at the bottom of Siberia. This expanse of loose sand posed little danger to players, and rugger offered a new and challenging diversion.

Plenty of novices came forward to learn the game and it was not long before Second Mate Ray Eddy had organized the six nascent teams into a rugby league. Soon the famous names Barbarians, Harlequins, Hornets, Old Watsonians, Saracens and Wasps were on everybody's lips. And the emblems of those revered teams were made and proudly worn by their Milag counterparts.

Later, an international league was formed and the ancient rivalries, never far below the veneer of camp life, added zest to the game. As Harold Simpson – himself a keen player – noted in his Log at the time 'The majority of the camp had never seen Rugby played before, so it speaks well of the game that it had such a following – even if they only came to see the spectacle of the loose scrum, yelling such encouragements as, "Kick him to death'", "Chew his ear off", and so on'.

The cricket scene in Milag was as utterly unlike the idealized English village green as one could possibly imagine. At first the game was played on the cinder-sandy surface of the *Platz*, surrounded by grim barracks and often impeded by queues at the parcel office.

Despite the drawbacks, there was no lack of enthusiasm among the players or spectators; nor lack of ingenuity in improving the necessary equipment. Balls were made by winding Red Cross parcel string around a pebble core and finishing off the outside with a covering of 'fancy work' hitches, beloved of the seamen in the age of sail. Bats were carved out of wood, their lack of spring being offset by the softness of the balls. Pads were absolutely unobtainable in Hitler's Third Reich, either by love – of which we had none to give – or money – which was worthless – or by bribery and corruption – which we were prepared to apply ruthlessly. So, batsmen and wicket-keepers had to take a chance of a knock from a ball flying unpredictably off the uneven cinder surface.

A cricket group within the Milag Sports Organization promoted the game, and in the first (1942) season fielded no fewer than seventeen teams formed on a barrack basis. Subsequently the same method as that for composing soccer teams was adopted and ten more-evenly matched teams were formed for the 1943 season. These teams took the names of famous English cricketing counties and boasted a first and second division. Matches between Officers and Ratings, Engine Room v. Deck, were also keenly contested.

By the second season the Germans had prohibited the playing of ball games on the *Platz*, but were somehow persuaded to lay a strip of concrete in the loose sand of 'Siberia' to serve as a cricket pitch.

My own shipowners, Trinder, Anderson & Co. Ltd., generously provided us with a splendid set of cricket equipment. The concrete pitch soon tore a real cricket ball to bits as it came off the concrete at an alarming speed. To rectify this, matting composed of old blankets covered with the *'ersatz'* sacking of palliasses was laid on top of the concrete pitch and tied down to pegs in the sand; then it was found that a ball would not rise until the tension of the lacing was suitably adjusted. Naturally there was much controversy on this matter among the cognoscenti.

There was a pleasant lift to the camp's morale when, on odd occasions, the Germans permitted a match between a Milag team and our so-near-yet-so-far compatriots in Marlag.

With Aussies in the camp, naturally Test Matches were played, and partisanship reached a high pitch of excitement. As there were relatively few men from 'down under' from which to pick their team, their excellent performance was the more remarkable. A replica of the famous 'Ashes' trophy was carved by 'Chippy' Frensham and presented to the Australian Eleven for their plucky stand in 1942 and victory in the series in 1943. England claims they should have taken the Ashes home in 1944 because they won the first four matches played, but the series was not finished because of the developments in the world beyond the wire, so the Aussies held on to the trophy and to this day it is in the possession of their captain Vic Marks, at Albert Park, South Australia.

Whereas the Germans understood soccer and liked to watch our games, cricket mystified them. Why, only two men of one side were playing at a time, the other nine sitting down watching the game! *Ach, ich nicht verstehen!*

Life at sea did not favour the active pursuit of athletics, so few men in the camp had had any previous experience of running and jumping, etc. Yet a large number quickly became interested and by coaching and training developed into competent athletes.

A Grand Athletics Sports Day was organized for late August. To sharpen competition, prizes were given to the individual winners and points awarded, which were aggregated in inter-barrack and inter-national events.

Under the heading 'Athletic Argonauts', John Watson wrote an account of the event for The Camp (the controversial newspaper published by the Germans and distributed to prison camps throughout Germany). He began, 'If I had not seen it I could never have believed that such an efficiently-run Sports Day was possible in a prison camp, in this instance, Milag Nord, Westertimke, the present home of some 2,600 Merchant Seamen of the United Nations. By 12.30 we had taken our seats on the edge of the track laid down on the camp's main *platz* and heard the sound of bagpipe and drum as the procession of athletes and officials approached from an assembly point further down in the camp. Arriving on the *platz*, the procession led by the band and carrying standards denoting the various countries represented, duly amazed and gratified the spectators by its sartorial no less than its marching perfection. In fact, whilst it is common knowledge that the Merchant Navy make a point of knowing nothing about drill, it came as a distinct shock to see so many immaculate pairs of well-pressed trousers in the camp. It was this phenomenon that almost prevented us from noticing that the officials were wearing very professional-looking rosettes for the occasion.

'The competitors having adjourned to their enclosure, and the officials and stewards to their respective places on the field, it was noticed that the High Command, who invariably displayed some interest in our recreational activities had arrived and taken their places a few minutes before the "off" of the first event – the 100 yards Championship.'

A full programme of races and field events occupied the whole afternoon. There were some wry smiles when the heavy-weight team, composed mostly of staff from the Galley and Hospital, won the tug-of-war. An outstanding gymnastic display was given by Ted Farringdon and his five-man team. There was cricket ball throwing and 'novelty' items – a sack race, an egg and spoon race and an obstacle race – which created so much hilarity that even the grim-looking barracks around the *Platz* seemed to take on a kindlier air.

Following a break for tea – and the inevitable *appel* – the Orama Band gave a lively start to the evening session which included the finals of several inter-barrack events and, the highlight of the day, the final of the international half-mile Medley Relay Race. Australia, Canada, Ireland, Wales and the West Indies had been eliminated in the preliminary heats, leaving Norway, Scotland and England to battle it out in the final over distances of 440, 220 and 2 x 110 yards.

Norway was fancied by some because one of its team had run in the 1936 Olympics, but the English team with Albert Kendall placed to do the final 110 yards sprint were the overall favourites.

The evening sun bathed the *Platz* in a golden light. Competitors in their white outfits, with national emblems displayed on their breasts, took up their stations, each in his lane clearly marked with silver sand. Spectators jostling for favourite positions, were buzzing with excitement.

There was a hush when the starter took up his position with whistle to lips (the Germans wouldn't trust us with a pistol!). The first three runners crouched on their marks, tendons taut. A roar of support broke out from the sidelines as the whistle shrilled and the runners raced away on the 440 yards leg, Joe Barratt in the lead. Then a groan went up, as Joe dropped his baton. He skidded to a halt, turned, clawed up the baton and with miraculous agility resumed the race. He was thirty yards behind when he handed the baton to Zimmerman, who made up twenty yards, evoking a great response from the crowd. 'Beetle' Harrison managed to retain his position and, taking a perfect pass, Albert Kendall started the last lap ten yards astern of the formidable Viking, Ole Johansen, who was leading the field. The spectators – Germans and all – were in a frenzy of excitement, yelling their heads off as, stride by stride, Albert caught up to win by a foot.

So ended a great race and a memorable Sports Day. The world about us looked rosier that evening.

Boxing was a sport that had always interested many seafarers. For those handy with gloves there were opportunities in many ports around the world for a contest at short notice. One recalls the famous Canon Brady of the Mission to Seamen in Buenos Aires, coming aboard to invite men to 'boxing and biffing at the Mission tonight', and not a few hard cases took a hiding from the reverend Canon himself.

In Milag, there were a number of experienced boxers, some of whom had professional status, so it was not surprising that they took the earliest opportunity to pursue and promote the sport. They had to contend with primitive training facilities and improvised equipment as best they could, but there was no lack of aspiring pugilists. By autumn 1942 the old hands, and especially Tommy Barham, sometime Light Weight Champion of the 'Old Ring', Blackfriars, had trained a number of youngsters up to the standard sufficiently high to warrant the promotion of a major tournament.

It was a fine Sunday in September. A ring had been built in the middle of the *Platz* and barracks had been emptied of forms and stools to provide seating around the ring. Lots had been drawn to decide the allocation of seats amongst the barracks. The British and German 'top brass' were taking up their privileged ring-side seats, and the common run of spectators were finding their places in their barrack allotment. It was an animated scene, and the Orama Band was playing lively numbers which created a carnival atmosphere that momentarily dispelled the gloom of captivity. Contestants and their trainers were making their final preparations in the nearby officers' washroom.

At one o'clock precisely, 'Bish' Rowcroft, our endearing extrovert compere, took the ring in an immaculate white tropical uniform and began to review the programme, interspersing his remarks with ribald wisecracks. Then he introduced the first contestants and the tournament got under way, with several well-fought bouts between the up-and-coming youngsters.

The applause for the last of these had scarcely stopped when 'Bish' announced the star contest of the day: Lloyd 'Kid' Hartley, the negro professional welterweight champion of Jamaica, versus the white Fred West, sometime heavyweight champion of the West India Station. They were to fight ten rounds, and a lot of *Lager Geld* was staked on this match. It was a close contest with the more experienced and heavier West trying to land one fearful blow on his elusive opponent. The clever West Indian was not caught and his fast counter-punching earned him a points decision. But it was touch and go. The crowd was in a fever of excitement until the last bell and it was rather an anti-climax to have to retrieve furniture and return to barracks.

It was the Canadians, not least the priests, who got Milag on skates. When the fire pond froze over, ingenious minds cast about for suitable material from which to make skates. Sharp eyes spotted the strap hinges on certain black-out shutters, and it was not long before they were spirited away and converted into practical though unconventional skates. As the sport caught on and demand for skates increased, our 'businessmen' rose to the occasion and obtained, by means never questioned, an adequate supply.

Soon the ambition to form teams and play ice hockey called for a more extensive rink. A flat site at the bottom of Siberia was pegged out and carefully levelled. When a good hard frost had set in it was watered and the frost sealed the sandy surface. The whole expanse was then flooded so as to form a coat of ice several inches thick and smooth enough for skating. The nearest water supply was in the washroom of Barrack 34. A pipe was made of dozens of KLIM tins (lids and bottoms removed) and used to convey water to an open drain running downhill towards the site. Another KLIM tin pipe led it to the rink.

Before the winter of 1942/43 was out the Merchant Navy on the touchlines had acquired a taste for a new sport and was beginning to appreciate some of the finer points of the incredibly fast game. They learned something about baseball, too, for the North Americans naturally enough wished to enjoy their national sport. Once the window-free *'sportsplatz'* down in Siberia was opened they could safely indulge in it.

For weeks on end, no outdoor games could be played and table tennis came into its own. It needed a minimum of equipment, all of which, except balls, could be made within the camp from materials available or procurable by cunning at low expense. Championship matches were organized and supervised by the M.S.O.

It goes almost without saying that even the rich variety of activities, so far described, did not satisfy the needs of every temperament and taste in the camp. Whether we seafarers who had been more than somewhat subjected to 'the changes and chances of this fleeting world' were more prone to gambling than landsmen would be hard to determine. The fact is that games of chance, and taking a gamble on games, were prevalent at all seasons.

One of the most reputable groups that set out to satisfy this urge to 'have a flutter' in a pleasant and sociable way was styled the Milag Jockey Commission. A horse race game on a grand scale, a variation on that still played on cruise ships, was created. The 'course' was laid on the tops of tables placed end to end and arranged to run the whole length of the Officers' Hall. The course was divided into lanes and each lane was divided at short intervals along its length. Realistic looking horses with jockeys mounted and sporting various 'owners' colours were cut out of plywood from Red Cross packing cases. These cut-outs, fixed on blocks of wood to keep them upright, were moved by their owners on the throw of a dice.

Betting was done on the totalizator principle, with the 'clerks' indicating the odds in some mysterious way by manipulating ping-pong balls threaded on strings.

The Jockey Commission became quite rich in time and was responsible for a number of benefactions, such as trophies for sports events. One purchase of trophies at bargain prices was made quite properly through the German authorities, who obtained them from a sports shop in Hamburg, which had been wrecked by the R.A.F.

Some men began to make 'parlour-games' in the very earliest days of their captivity; indeed, they would start, as if by instinct, as soon as they could lay hands on any serviceable material and tools. Dominoes, draughts and chess, because of the relative ease of making them from cardboard with a pocket knife and pencil, were among the first games to be produced; dice were not far behind.

In the sophisticated society of Milag there were devotees of all the usual indoor pastimes. Card games of all sorts ranging from the solemnities of bridge through whist to out and out gambling games were played, and, as already indicated, so were the board games of chess, draughts and backgammon. Popular, too, was the more complex mah-jong, a strange symbol of the Far East to fetch up in *deutsche gefangenschaft*. Conventional games of chance also flourished. They ranged from those with a mechanical basis like roulette, to dice, poker and others using cards.

In the drab monotony which, month by month, was 'life' for so many, I suppose the mild excitement at the gaming tables was therapeutic. And I heard of only one man who went to the length of selling essentials to enable him to follow the gambler's wild dream of breaking the bank.

As in the real world, the promoters and bookmakers were the men who got rich. Of this clan the most famous was Kenji (Jimmy) Takaki, a Liverpudlian of Japanese extraction. Riches in this connection were in the form of *Lager Geld*, and although we paid £1 for 10 Camp Marks, they were, when taken by the handful, practically valueless for there was nothing much to buy. But Jimmy, having the means, discovered ways through our gaolers of making purchases and in the course of time this generous man acquired a harmonium for the R.C. chapel and two pianos for the theatre.

At most sporting events in the camp bookies were on hand to lay the odds and with stands, boards and rollicking names like 'Genuine Jimmy', they looked like the real thing. *Lager Geld* flowed freely, mostly in to the bookies' pockets.

The Germans also became very interested in our outdoor games, especially soccer matches, and some of them took every permitted opportunity to watch the play. I never heard prisoners object to their presence; it could scarcely have failed to mellow their general attitude toward us.

The benefit of these sporting activities to us was undoubtedly great. Players, of course, got themselves into better physical and mental trim than they otherwise might have done. The effect on spectators varied from the uplift on enthusiasts, critically interested in finer points of play, to the therapeutic action on the mind of a fellow who was down in the dumps. It was fitting that good players who contributed so much to the pleasure and well-being of their campmates, should enjoy a degree of hero-worship. Besides this general acclaim the M.S.O. awarded shields to teams winning the big events and medals to the player. Yes, medals, shining and silvery, designed and made in the camp! The M.S.O. awarded an impressive-looking diploma to each player in the major team events, and to individual winners of athletics, boxing and such like competitions. The M.S.O. certainly served the camp very well indeed and it earned and enjoyed the gratitude of all hands.

CHAPTER ELEVEN

Food For Thought

It would be difficult to overrate the value and importance of educational activities for men subjected to enforced idleness in our circumstances. Whilst unaccustomed leisure could seduce a man to stray along the path of indolence to boredom, depression and far worse, the circumspect recognized it as a golden opportunity for study that might never recur in a lifetime. Great credit is therefore due to the public-spirited ones who, with Mr. Johns, endured with patience the inevitable delays and frustrations involved in initiating and sustaining suitable courses of study for them.

Living, as we were, in an 'unprofessional' community, the emphasis was on the teaching of nautical subjects. Many of the younger men had only just begun their professional studies. Others of us hadn't yet obtained all of our 'tickets'. Among the former group were about forty apprentices whose individual sea-time ranged from that of 17-year-old Norman Calvert, who had hardly got his sea legs on his first voyage when SCHARNHORST sank his ship in mid-Atlantic, to seniors nearly out of their 'time'. Captain T. W. Morris pioneered the first classes in seamanship and navigation for the apprentices 'to keep the boys out of mischief', as he put it.

Other courses in nautical subjects for Mates and Engineers were soon launched. These included Naval Architecture and Ship Construction, Meteorology, Mathematics and Mechanics, even First-Aid; all as required by the examining authorities at home. It was amusing that courses in radio technology were *verboten* by our gaolers.

All of these courses were designed to give students the opportunity of pursuing their professional studies up to, and usually beyond, the standard set by the Board of Trade, which was the examining body in this instance. So, with his heart set on release from captivity some day, a man could school himself to take an exam at the earliest moment after regaining blessed freedom. Unfortunately the student could not, while a prisoner, build up 'sea-time', that is the time afloat on ship's Articles in a certain capacity, that had to be accumulated to qualify a candidate to sit for examination[1].

Of course, there were many men who had no reason to undertake the studies just mentioned, yet wished to follow a dream of qualifying for a 'shore job', or study something just because they saw it as a good thing to occupy their minds in an academic way. These needs found expression in classes for the German, French, Spanish and, for a while Norwegian languages. And there was a course in English Literature tutored by Padre Ball. Interest in Astronomy, natural enough among navigators, became a subject of more general interest in the spring of 1943, when a comet could be observed with the naked eye for many nights on end. Mr. Harker kept track of it and could always point out its position.

In the course of time, that is to say, the naturally lengthy period between making a request in Milag and receiving a book parcel in reply, many of us were able to pursue studies on our own account in subjects not in general demand, or that could not be initiated in a class for lack of room. Only two rooms, in Barrack 17, were reserved for both classes and private study, so it was a marvel of organization and discipline that so much work was done successfully in them.

In addition to participating in the nautical studies offered in the school, I wished to keep at least a toe-hold in the job I had left and which was kept open for me to go back to in peacetime. To this end I asked for a book on Industrial Gas Engineering and another on Engineering Metallurgy which had been a speciality of mine. Some months later the valuable tomes arrived bearing the stamp 'GIFT OF THE WAR ORGANIZATION OF BRITISH RED CROSS SOCIETY AND ORDER OF ST. JOHN OF JERUSALEM'.

Once again I am privileged to pay tribute to, and give heartfelt thanks for the wonderful work of those organizations which, in co-operation with the Universities and other British educational institutions and publishers, underpinned practically the whole of the

---

[1]*There was some easement of the rule at the end of the war when an allowance of one month's 'sea-time' was made for every six months in captivity, up to a maximum of six months' 'sea-time'.*

invaluable educational activities within the Camp.

Closely allied to academic study as a means of profitably occupying and exercising the mind, was reading. At first there were but few books in Milag, and one was occasionally amazed to discover among them British books of former times that had been printed on the Continent in the English Language and had somehow gravitated into the camp. I came across a copy of Macaulay's **History of England from the Accession of James II**, and I also read a copy of Johnson's 'Rambler' essays which had been printed in 1820.

By degrees, books began to arrive from Britain in private parcels from friends, relatives and generous shipowners. When the original recipients had finished with them they tended to be circulated among friends. It was at this stage that the Library came into existence, and in true Milag style it was quickly organized and efficiently run by Eric Ackland, much to the benefit of our wire-bound community.

An exhibition of handicrafts held in the summer of 1942 confirmed that ship model-making was a natural occupation of imprisoned mariners. There were tiny full-riggers sailing forever over stormy seas under lowering skies in their little bottles; and many fine scale models of 'my last ship', wrought with skill, patience and affection, were fitting memorials to ships that now lived only in men's memories. Viewers of these works who were familiar with the exquisite models made of bone by French sailors imprisoned in England during the Napoleonic wars might wonder about our different diets, for we never saw a bone fit for model making.

There were rings, ornaments and statuettes cast of aluminium, which commanded attention, not only for their form and finish but for the fact that such castings could have been made in the camp. There was no secret as to where the metal came from, for there were various utensils, containers and wrappings of aluminium about the place that could be used. The mystery was about the equipment and method devised to generate the necessary heat from our slow-burning briquettes to melt the metal. In fact the miniature furnaces with their hand-powered fans to supply the air-blast would have made fascinating exhibits in their own right – had we dared to show them. The moulds were generally made of the German-issued soap, and this was the only really satisfactory use we ever found for the stuff.

The furnace itself, in which the melting pot was placed on the fuel bed, was made of a large German jam tin lined with clay to resist the heat. Clay, incidentally, had had to be imported to line the fire ponds. The necessary air blast was derived from a paddle-wheel type of rotary fan. A KLIM tin formed its casing, and the air from it was blown into the furnace through a conveniently-sized long thin biscuit tin. The fan was hand-driven by a belt running round a fairly large wooden wheel, mounted separately from the fan, and a small bobbin on one end of the fan spindle. Bunk board had to be sacrificed to make the wheel and base for the whole apparatus. The webbing of British Army trouser braces was considered to be the best material for the belt!

Drawings and paintings naturally made a good showing because art materials could be obtained a little more easily than others through Dr. Blancke, whose enigmatic role appeared to include our 'kultural' welfare.

There was an intriguing dart board, cunningly made of thousands of dead matches bundled together to form a conventional circular board upon which the usual divisions and numbers were marked.

There were also some commendable wood carvings, some needlework, tapestry and peg rugs. An exhibit which kindled a poignant response was a half-finished clock in wood left by our late comrade Walter Skett.

Our little show aroused general admiration, even amongst those Germans who were permitted to see it – with the exception of our bête noire Güsfeld, whose nasty mind speculated on how we had got hold of and retained tools suitable for doing such work. No doubt it wounded his professional pride that he and his sleuths had not discovered and confiscated them on one of their searches.

Even in our spartan world it was amazing how many useful materials there were to hand, or could be procured by guile; and the number of uses to which they were put was equally astonishing.

The use of Red Cross parcel string for theatrical wigs and cricket balls has been mentioned already. Its other uses were legion. Obviously it could serve as boot laces and for any common tying-up job. Being fairly thick, and strong, it was very satisfactory for making many sorts of network; for example, football goal nets, tennis nets, and cricket practice nets. Hammocks were another form of network to be seen about the camp occasionally in the summertime.

When three strands were plaited in the simplest way it was used for clothes lines. When plaited more elaborately into the form that sailors call square sennit, other possibilities opened up. Rope soles were made of it, which could be sewn on to the uppers of worn-out shoes to convert them into slippers or dry-weather footwear. An elaboration of this design was used for running shoes, made by the incorporation of broad-headed felt nails (stolen from carpenters re-felting a barrack roof) in the soles with spikes projecting outward and heads sandwiched between stout cardboard to hold them in place and protect the feet of the athlete. Square sennet was often used for making door mats of more or less intricate design, and as we had a very sandy soil, they were an effective aid to keeping our rooms clean.

The stout cardboard Red Cross food parcel boxes were also a great asset. Every man had a few of these in which to store his food and few belongings. The cardboard made good innersoles for boots; covers for notebooks when we had to make our own; various table games and tie-on labels. In the theatre they were invaluable in the making of scenery and various stage properties.

Sometimes the Red Cross parcels were delivered to the camp in chests made of plywood. Most of this material went to the theatre, but some was released to the camp in general. At one time it was the 'in thing' for theatre-goers to own portable back rests that some genius had designed to fit on the forms that constituted the seating in the auditorium. The same idea was applied to the wooden stools in our rooms to convert them into more comfortable chairs.

The leather tongues of old boots had their uses: watch straps, coat toggles, glove facings, trouser bottom wear-reducers, purses, wallets and belts. Belts were made by cutting small pieces into figure-of-eight shapes, folding each piece in half, then linking them together to form a chain.

If a patient man is hell-bent on doing a job of soldering, it is remarkable how much solder metal he can accumulate by collecting the small air-seal blobs on tobacco tins, and scraping the soldered seams that are on the side of most food cans. Resinous flux was to hand on the fir trees in the camp.

Aluminium foil, and various containers and small objects of that metal, were the source of material used for casting a variety of objects such as sports medals and other trophies, badges and fittings for ice skates. While German soap was an excellent material from which to make small moulds, clay was used for larger work.

A less salubrious activity that engaged the talents of some of our fellows was the production and distillation of alcohol, the end product glorying in a number of names from commonplace booze or hooch to alki. Potato peelings, which were supposed to be taken 'outside' to feed local pigs, were a prime raw material. In times of opulence, raisins, prunes and other dried fruits might be used and, in season, apples would be smuggled in to put in the mash. The Germans did their best to stamp out this illegal activity, so there was a premium on stills that would escape detection.

One elementary outfit that I came across is worth describing for its ingenuity and simplicity. A big German jam tin was used to contain a certain amount of the fermented liquor and when in operation this container would be stood on the bogey to simmer. A piece of brick was stood in the liquor, its top clear of the surface of the liquid. On the brick was stood a small receptacle – perhaps half of a condensed milk tin. Finally, a standard hemispherical German bowl, about the size of a small colander, would be set into the open top of the jam tin. In use the bowl was kept full of cold water, so when the vapour was given off from the liquor it would condense on the cold, curved underside of the bowl, gravitate to the lowest point and drip into the receptacle standing on the brick. Q.E.D.!

As time went on and tinsmithing skills were developed, stills of a more intricate design and sophisticated construction came into use. Furthermore, one got the impression that our captors began to tolerate the practice to a certain extent on the assumption that we might otherwise get up to some other mischief that would cause them more trouble.

The whole process and the ethos of its operation is nicely summarized in the following Milag doggerel of anonymous authorship which is preserved in Bill Errington's Log Book.

'ALKI' IN OTHER WORDS 'HOOCH'

Take some Red X raisins, anyone's will do,
Also prunes and sugar, and we'll make a dinkum brew.
Knock a kleine barrel and in it we will cram
All the junk together along with Jerry Jam.

Now top it up with water, a couple of quarts at least,
And finally work the firkin with an ounce or two of yeast.
Stick it in the corner close behind the stove
And very soon the prunes will all begin to move.

Up and down together, like corks upon a tide
And by tomorrow morning all hell's let loose inside,
And leave her quietly standing for close upon a week
And while the 'divils' brewing, a Jack and Jill we'll seek.

Find a nice new jam tin with a closely fitting top,
A lot of pipes and little tins to cook the maddening pop.
Just solder these together with true gefangener skill
And by the time you've finished, you'll have a damned good still.

And now the job is finished, we'll stand it on the stove
And start brewing the doings the kind we 'geffies' love.
It'll take about ten minutes to warm the hooch pot up
So stand by with your spoons to try a little sup.
Hear the glad rejoicing 'Saints and Sinners' shout
'Stick around you booze bums, the alki's coming out'.

Chapter Twelve

The Watershed

On a dark night in November, 1942, while tramping to and fro on the *Platz*, Bjørn Egge suddenly confided in me that he and some other Norwegians would soon attempt an escape. They would get out through a tunnel which was nearly completed. This news went through me like an electric shock and galvanized all my latent interest in regaining my freedom. We talked the matter over feverishly until the curfew warned us into our barracks. That night I could hardly sleep for the excitement of wildly adventurous thoughts.

At subsequent meetings he showed me a map of North-west Germany, copied from a motorists' guide, and an ingenious luminous compass which had been made in the camp.

Perhaps the most stirring piece of news was Bjørn's disclosure that Einar Sørensen, also from the Gothenburg ships, had escaped and had actually reached England. It was common knowledge that in the spring Sørensen had made a clever break from a party of prisoners from Milag in transit to Wilhelmshaven for interrogation. He had simply spilled out of the file of prisoners into the crowd of passengers on Bremen's main railway station. But in spite of the advantages of his civilian clothes, fluency in the German language and knowledge of the country, to say nothing of his courage, bad luck and hunger finally drove him to give himself up to the police in Hamburg. He was hauled back to Westertimke and condemned to two weeks' solitary confinement, after which he was packed off to a high-security camp in East Germany under armed guard.

The next news of him to reach Milag was in a letter to a friend, written by a lady and posted by ordinary P.O.W. mail in Britain. In Norwegian and ingeniously worded, the letter conveyed to us that Sørensen had given his guard the slip somewhere near Berlin and that he had made his exit by a Baltic port, but precisely which one of several possibilities was tantalizingly uncertain. Quite inexplicably, the Germans had again transported him dressed in civilian clothing.

Sørensen's success naturally heartened Bjørn and his friends and I saw it as a challenge.

Further discussion with Bjørn revealed that the would-be escapers had only the sketchiest plan of action for when they emerged from the tunnel. One would head for Bremen, another Bremerhaven another Hamburg, and so on. Beyond that they would simply take what chance offered. The thought struck me that some idea of conditions in our neighbourhood could be got from prisoners who worked outside the camp. So, with Bjørn's agreement, and without disclosing the Norwegian's designs, I took Harry Gray, AUSTRALIND's Chief Steward, into my confidence. He had worked on a local farm for several months and he was an astute fellow, so it was reasonable to suppose he could help us. I was right. Infected by my enthusiasm, he imparted a wealth of detailed information and even mooted the possibility of buying or stealing clothes and bicycles.

At this stage my zest for adventure was outgrowing my natural prudence, and with the added inducement of continuing fine weather I was on the point of asking Bjørn to let me go with him. He and his partners were keyed up for the enterprise. The tunnel was going well. Measurements indicated that the end was already just under the wire. Then luck deserted them. In the sandy earth, exactly under the path on which the sentries patrolled, they struck a rock. The sounds of their attempts to dig it out attracted the attention of the guard on that still night. So ended the first Milag tunnel.

After this anti-climax we had leisure for sober reflection on the situation. For me the experience was a watershed; I was determined to escape. With this whiff of freedom in our nostrils there was no thought of giving up.

Winter weather came upon us early in the New Year, compelling us to settle down to camp life with as much patience as we could muster, yet providing ample time to mull over schemes and puzzle our heads with their practical details.

My immediate task was to copy Bjørn's map. To do that secretly was not easy. To use the table in my room with fifteen others in the way was impossible. The study room – the only one for the whole camp at that date – was the only place in which I could do the job. There, in a position that couldn't be overlooked, I worked whenever it was safe to do so. Through the boot job I had acquired sheets of thin paper and a sheet of carbon paper. These, with the map on top, were pinned to a board (a locker shelf) ready for tracing. There was also an innocent drawing which could be folded down quickly in case of emergency. The map was duly traced in outline on the undersheets, then inked in, coloured and named. An outline map of Hamburg was treated in a similar fashion. It was a long and tedious job with many anxious moments.

I kept up my busy routine of activities and, I hoped, maintained an appearance of normality. There was the daily attendance at the 'bootery', Mr. Coventry's excellent classes on naval architecture and ship construction, Padre Ball's English Literature study group, the church choir, meteorology lectures and private study of the Norwegian and German languages.

The discovery of the tunnel gave the prisoners plenty to talk about, and the luckless Norwegians, for whom secrecy had been paramount, did not relish the limelight. But their notoriety was useful to me. When I had an opportunity to buy a French pocket compass from one of the Camp traders he immediately assumed that I was acting for my Norwegian friends and I did not disabuse him. One never asked where such contraband came from, but at this time of comparative opulence in cigarettes it was most likely smuggled in as a good saleable article by one of the Dutch carpenters who were erecting some additional barracks. For me it was a great treasure and a fascinating thing to keep on my person.

With the sickening feeling of helplessness that unheralded changes in our life produced, the Norwegians received a peremptory order to leave the camp on 3rd February, 1943. No-one knew their destination. The optimists believed they were being repatriated. Otto Brunes was not so confident, and asked me to let him have any blue gabardine raincoat in case a chance of escape occurred during the journey. The possible consequences of my refusal, on the grounds that I would need it myself, for even Otto didn't know my intentions, haunted me for a long time. It was sad to be parted from that fine body of young patriots, especially my particular friends, Bjørn and

Otto.

The more thought I gave to the problem the clearer it became that there were certain requirements that ought to be fulfilled before I left the camp, to shorten the odds for success. Besides maps and the compass that I had so fortunately acquired, physical fitness – really hard condition, not just good health – was essential. Adequate disguise for whatever role I decided to adopt, a cache of food in the right place and personal acquaintance with the German world outside the wire all were important. It occurred to me that all could be acquired at a stroke, simply by taking a job on a local farm. Of course, officers, who were not compelled to work, were not in the habit of 'working for the bloody Germans'. The few who did so, for reasons of health or to preserve their sanity were regarded with extreme disfavour, if not open hostility, by the rest.

I was quite ready to bear the opprobrium of my many friends who would not know my motive. More worrying was that, knowing me as they did, and well aware of my attitude towards our captors, they might start speculating as to what I was up to and generate rumours that could reach the Germans and make me a marked man. So I decided to prepare the way for this step well in advance. Being the 'king pin' in the boot repair service, I was approached from time to time for special attention to 'farmers' boots by Gordon Shaw, whose unenviable task it was to procure any labour force legitimately demanded by the Germans. At a suitable moment I intimated to him, half jokingly, how bored I was becoming with the monotony of camp life and that when spring came I would ask him for a job on a farm. Having heard of the strenuous nature of the work on the local peasant holdings I deemed it wise to get my name on the list of those willing to work on a camp vegetable garden which was to start when the better weather arrived. That course, I hoped, would break me in to physical labour gently as well as wean me from my camp activities in an unobtrusive way.

At this date there were certain British officers constituting an 'escape committee' in another barrack than mine, but after making discreet enquiry into their activities and methods, I decided not to ask if I might join them. Where prison life was not intolerable it was easy to fall into the error of mistaking escapism for the real thing, and it may be a consequence of this that men incline towards tunnel digging. The titillation of the sense of adventure may be spread over several months and carry with it the pleasure of laughing up one's sleeve at the Germans the whole time. No doubt there are prisons where a tunnel is the only practical way of getting out, but in our circumstances it seemed a gross waste of time and effort and the result less certain than the simple operation of walking out of the gate with German approval. So, my decision to get a farm job and use the gate disposed of the first of the three main problems that an escaper had to tackle. The other two were how to reach a suitable port or frontier and how to get out of German territory with a whole skin.

Since the departure of the Norwegians, Harry Gray was my only confidant. One of the difficulties about planning an escape in Milag was that of maintaining secrecy. This arose from the fact that the 3,000 or so prisoners comprised a couple of dozen nationalities. With the exception of a handful of passengers, all were merchant seamen and, having so much in common, there was a great underlying unity. But with such a mixed crew, including unfortunate citizens of occupied countries, it was not surprising that the Germans found, or forcibly created, a stooge or two. An experience concerning such a simple matter as my illegal possession of two plovers' eggs gave me timely warning of this petty espionage. So, secrecy must be the watchword, with no person unnecessarily informed of my intentions nor given cause to start guessing at them. Nevertheless, new sources of information had to be found. This situation led me to divulge my intentions to Captain Carr, whom I had grown to like and respect as a man with an astute and lively mind. He was in a position to glean information from the 'top brass' in the camp, without arousing suspicion; furthermore, on clothing business he sometimes met his 'opposite number' in Marlag, our neighbouring Royal Naval prisoners' camp with which we had few contacts.

This spring was a time when hope in our hearts began to outweigh despair. The Eighth Army was routing the vaunted Afrika Korps. Stalingrad had been relieved and the Russians were driving the Nazis out of the Caucasus. These momentous events had repercussions even in our little world. Our guards were noticeably

April 24th 1943.

Mr. Bird.

Dear Sir,

May we express our appreciation of your service to the Lamp in the organizing and running of the boot repair dept.

We regret your going but realize that a change of employment from time to time is most desirable and we sincerely hope that you will derive much benefit from your new occupation.

Yours Faithfully
Joh. Iles. (Sec)

Ratings Welfare Committee.

less cock-a-hoop. Many of the more able-bodied ones had been drafted to more active service and most of their replacements were elderly or far down the scale of physical fitness. The dread of being sent to the Eastern Front weighed on them all and we did nothing to relieve them. Our winter had been less severe than the previous one. Red Cross food parcels and private mail arrived fairly regularly; and all the camp activities were flourishing.

For 'private reasons' I handed over the job in the Bootery to my stalwart colleague and friend, Tom Cockburn. I must admit I was touched when I received the following letter from the Ratings' Welfare Committee.

I never kept a diary in Milag except for this period when I was planning to escape from it. The notebook in which I did make a few entries has survived and the following quotations from it will awaken memories in any of my old camp-mates who chance to read them and may allow others some inkling of our strange wartime community.

Sunday, 28th March, 1943

Announcement of additional *appel* and changed times. From Monday there will be three (instead of two) musters daily: at 7.00 a.m.; 1.00 p.m. and 6.00 p.m.

Inspected by Kommandant Hensel! We feel the chains on such occasions. Bacon and meat roll pie for tea with a crust made by Albert Gillis.

Monday, 29th March, 1943

Soup time for non-communal messman 11.00-11.30 a.m. Mid-day *appel* 12.45-1.10 p.m., not as bad as anticipated. Feldwebel Müller returned from leave, got an ovation.

To the Indian theatre 6.30 p.m. Enjoyed the sequel to 'King Akbar'. There was some really good acting. Well applauded.

Mr. Harker pointed out the comet's new position. It had moved a great deal since I first saw it.

Tuesday, 30th March, 1943

Called on Rashid and congratulated him on the Indian Show. He pressed me to a cup of sweet tea and a dried banana.

Went to a concert 'Mine own Countree', a programme of music and song by A. Hopkins, rendered by the Orama Band and the Chordites. A fine performance.

Wednesday, 31st March, 1943

Out on Camp vegetable garden digging: 8.30-11.00 a.m.

Thursday, 1st April, 1943

Jock (John Andrews, my combine mate) tried to make an April Fool of me. On *appel* he said in a serious tone, 'There's no tea in the tin,' but I wasn't caught. Jock, Alf (Holmes) and I 'soogied' out our corner of the room and bunks, being the day for clean linen. Talked with Captain Carr on 'our subject'.

Friday, 2nd April, 1943

On garden raking 8.30-11.00 a.m.

Read Darwin's account of Condors in dinner hour.

Bathed in lower wash-house after *appel*; top one flooded.

Lights on upper camp circuit failed at 9.30 p.m.

Saturday, 3rd April, 1943

9.30 a.m. Literary Group meeting. Mr. Douglas read a short paper on Pope.

1.30-2.30 p.m. Mr. Coventry's lecture (ship construction) on stern frames in twin screw ships.

Sunday, 4th April, 1943

Washed my clothes before joining the party of 24, mostly from my Barrack 15, at the gate at 10.25 a.m. We set out for Lager 4 at 10.39 a.m. and marched there in fifteen minutes. A pleasant jaunt on a fine spring morning. Saw Beverly (one of the Deck Boys on my ship) working on his farm en route. Underwent X-ray examination for T.B. and passed as O.K. Arrived back in Milag 11.49 a.m. After tea, reading 'The Rambler', this copy printed in 1820 brought in camp by Harry Gray. 7.00 p.m. choir practice.

Tuesday, 6th April, 1943
   8.30-10.45 a.m. on Camp garden, four of us raking. Several heavy showers and squalls – one blew off a section of Barrack 23 roof. We saw it happen from the shelter of a garage. Several heavy hailstorms today – large stones, conical shape.

Thursday, 8th April, 1943
   After 6.00 p.m. *appel* watched Wolves v. Preston North End football match.

Friday, 9th April, 1943
   Worked (with John Weston, the scenery artist) at the theatre the whole day making paper foliage ceiling-breaking festoons for the cave scene (for the 'Desert Song').
   The 'peggy' put on 'straff' for smoking on *appel*.

Saturday, 10th April, 1943
   An hour's cricket practice at the back of the South washroom.

Tuesday, 13th April, 1943
   At theatre making stars. Called on Dr. Hallam, thinking to give him a trim up. He was asleep – over-eating some said!

Wednesday, 14th April, 1943
   At theatre; gilding round archway in harem set.
   I saw my first butterfly of the year on the 1.00 p.m. *appel*. The warm humid air of this beautiful April day had brought it out, and as we stood there it fluttered golden-white over the apex of the galley roof. In keen expectation I waited to see if it would re-appear. Sure enough, through the straight fir trunks it went, flitting on until the canteen screened it from my view.

Saturday, 17th April, 1943 (this is the last entry)
   Saw the first dress rehearsal of the 'Desert Song'; at least, until all the scenes had been shown.
   Witnessed a thrilling sight on the 1.00 p.m. *appel* – a daylight raid by the R.A.F. over the Bremen area. Large bombers, intrepidly

maintaining correct stations, flew on and majestically wheeled among the black puffs of shell bursts and curving white streaks of fighter plane exhausts.

Chapter Thirteen

Setting Course For Freedom

The camp vegetable garden project was coming along nicely. Its site was only a couple of hundred yards outside the camp gate and in full view of it; nevertheless, the hours spent there in the open tilling the soil were a golden foretaste of the freedom I longed for.

On 3rd May, 1943, I awoke early and went out to hear the 'dawn chorus'. It was all the more enjoyable because I had just read Earl Grey's **The Charm of Birds**, one of a number of books which our generous shipowners, Trinder, Anderson & Co. Ltd. had sent us. I spent the morning with the usual party on the garden. On returning for *'mittag-essen'* I heard that Gordon Shaw was anxious to see me. 'I've got a farm job for you,' he said, 'and I want you to go out at one o'clock.' This was thrilling news and it gave me a strange feeling inside.

After a hurried meal I went out to the gate to be booked out and to be given an escort. I was to be taken to Bauer Jan Michaelis's farm 29 at Kirktimke, the neighbouring village two kilometres away, whose church spire rising through the trees I had so often watched and whose bell-chimes I had heard ringing out over the countryside. It was a glorious spring day and delightful to be out. Soon we were past Lager 4, the furthest I had been away from the camp for many months.

The farm was located beside the church. A knock on the side door brought the farmer from his meal table. A gaunt figure, his powerful frame bowed by years of toil. Yet he was surprisingly young to be out of uniform. The guard explained that I was the new prisoner, dismissed himself and went back to the camp. Had I eaten lunch? When I assured the farmer that I had and refused any more, he went in, indicating that I should remain outside until the meal was finished. I then noticed a young woman sitting on the grass and with her two young men and children, all engaged in some rough play; mostly trying to steal her wooden clogs. I caught her name –

Stephania. She was a sturdy girl, obviously in her early twenties, flaxen-haired and attractive because of her vigorous health rather than her beauty. She was the first woman I had been near for nearly two years. The boys were the farmer's sons. One man was a prisoner from Milag, a Yugoslav who called himself Bozo, the other a Ukrainian 'slave worker' called Mico. The girl was a Pole and they spoke together in a Slav tongue which they all understood, except the boys to whom they spoke in Platt Deutch. I lay down apart, taking in this strange scene.

Eventually the farmer came out. It was the signal to start work and I was given to understand, through Bozo, that I should go with him. Instead of anything back-breaking, as I had anticipated, we went round the house to a clamp of potatoes. Here I met 'Alte 'Trina', a maiden aunt of the farmer's, a toothless old crone who laboured on the land with the rest. The afternoon quickly passed 'chitting' old potatoes and bagging them up. At 3.00 p.m. we repaired to the house and ate large thick slices of home-made rye bread with butter and 'jam', washed down with *ersatz* coffee, a somewhat pleasanter brew than that served in the camp, and we had milk with it. At 7.00 p.m. we finished for the day and ate the evening meal of fried potatoes, followed by 'milk soup'. Bozo and I assembled with the other 'farmers' (prisoners) at the church gate about 7.30 p.m. The guards arrived and we were marched 'home'. So I began my new life and the real training for *der tag*.

Farmer Jan Michaelis was a kindly man with no sympathy for the Nazis. He had been conscripted but played the half-witted yokel so well that he was discharged from the Army. I had nothing but good treatment from him and his family; so I hoped they would not be punished when I absconded. On Sunday mornings when 'farmers' went out of the camp only to get their morning meals – and to trade – I used to amuse the boys. Kallaheinz was just at the right age to appreciate the bows and arrows I made for him.

Timber sawing and chopping were but a foretaste of the hard labour to come. Bozo, who had some special reason for wishing to remain on this particular farm, worked like a demon. Jan Michaelis, himself, was one of the hardest workers I have ever seen and a good farmer too, which accounted for his place being about the best kept and most prosperous farm in the village. His pace took a bit of sticking, but in a month it hardened me up and, together with the wholesome, though coarse, diet, soon built up my strength and endurance.

Peat cutting for domestic fuel was done during May. Michaelis's strip of peat moor lay a mile or more from the village and somewhat on the other side from Milag. It was good to be alive those bright May days, the birch in young leaf and the fleecy clouds sailing across the blue sky. A few of the low grey roofs of Milag could be seen in the distance. One felt delightfully remote from it – that little world within a world. On one of these peat-cutting expeditions I had the opportunity in the lunch time to wander off alone into the neighbouring forest. Alone in the forest! What a strange feeling to be alone and to be somewhere I ought not to be!

It would be difficult to explain my presence if the Kommandant should suddenly appear riding on one of his hunting expeditions. A rare feeling indeed, and it gave me a valuable clue. One must be 'psychologically' prepared for escape; evidently I was not. I paid considerable attention to this aspect of the problem as time wore on.

Hay-making followed in June. It was satisfying to be out in the meadows tedding the rows of hay with a wooden rake in unison with the others. Old Aunt Trina was there too, in her old-fashioned poke bonnet, keeping the same rhythm as the rest of us.

It was hard work, for on this farm, as on all the local peasant holdings, there was no power-driven machinery. Carts were horse-drawn, and so was the grass-mower which was also used to cut the corn, but all the rest of the work was done by hand and, judged by British standards, in a most laborious manner.

For a Milagian the only promising way of escaping was by sea, preferably to neutral Sweden. Once at a German port, a seaman, one hoped, would feel more at home and able to tackle the problems of finding a ship and stowing away in her. The immediate difficulties concerned the choice of the best port to head for and deciding how to get to it.

Bremen was nearest, barely a day's march, but Sørensen had not got away from there, though he knew the place intimately. The docks were thought to be well-enclosed and presumably guarded.

Furthermore, I had no map of the city, nor could I determine whether Swedish ships visited the port regularly or not. Bremerhaven was more likely to be used, it was thought, but information about its present condition was completely lacking. Hamburg attracted me. I had been there before, I had a sketch map of the city and docks. And even if I failed to find a ship there, I was half-way to the Baltic ports, which seemed to offer the best chance of all. The big obstacle would be the river Elbe; doubtless the bridge to Hamburg would be well-policed. Harburg, till now, was just a name to me. I visualized it as a suburb of Hamburg on the south-west bank of the river. At this stage Captain Carr performed a valuable service by extracting useful information from Captain Cavaye (till recently the Camp Leader) about the port and disposition of its docks. The information thus gleaned was decisive in my choice of Harburg. A relatively small town and harbour, yet taking ocean-going vessels. The docks were said to be fairly accessible too. And it was on 'our' side of the river.

Naturally, a good deal of thought was given to the question as to which mode of travel to adopt. The options were to ride on the railway, march on foot or ride a bicycle – if I were lucky enough to get hold of one.

My map told me there was no direct railway from our district to Harburg, but a timetable I had 'acquired' indicated that the journey was possible by changing en route.

The distance by road was 50 miles; I reckoned that I could march it in two days. There seemed little doubt that the risk of being challenged and detected would be less on the roads, and the possibility of taking evasive action to avoid a tight corner would be greater.

The alternative had to be considered in the time scale I had set for the operation. This was based on food supply. I estimated that enough food could be carried conveniently to sustain me on low rations for five days, which period, plus two days of real starvation, ought to give me a fair chance to reach the port, find a ship and get away in her. So I decided to buy a degree of security at the cost of an extra day on the road and, perhaps, a pair of sore feet.

Harry Gray had stolen a pair of corduroy trousers for me, an excellent addition to my wardrobe. The intention was that I should be disguised as a German worker and wear such clothes that I would be inconspicuous in the country, in the town and on the dockside.

It became necessary once more to widen the circle of people in the know. This time, on Captain Carr's advice, I confided in Captain Bayot, a very intelligent and quick-witted Belgian, who had himself escaped from Belgium to Britain by way of France and Spain at the beginning of the war. His criticisms were invaluable; furthermore, he was able to introduce an entirely fresh element into the scheme. He had an 'outside contact' – a Belgian carpenter who was working in Germany and at that time was frequently in the camp itself. Although possibly a 'freewill' worker (i.e. a collaborator), he had befriended Bayot at considerable risk to himself by visiting the Captain's wife while on leave in Belgium. I took the chance and approached him for information about Harburg, Swedish shipping, Dock policing, passes and the like. He seemed willing to help. And when it was known that he had now brought his wife from Belgium who was living at a village in the market gardening district along the Elbe, new possibilities opened up. In fact, this development seemed the most important one so far.

Making contact with the Belgian, through Bayot, was a painfully slow and uncertain matter; sometimes he wouldn't come into the camp for days. Eventually a little information was collected and he was asked if he would be prepared to shelter me in his home in the event of a hue and cry over my escape, or to take me in for rest and recuperation if my first attempt to leave Harburg failed. The possibility of this refuge was very heartening and greatly raised my hopes of success.

After the first flush of spring the weather had become unsettled and got worse as the summer wore on. Fine weather was essential for my purpose, and there was no sign of it. The days of hard labour dragged slowly by. I was now fit and even getting stale. The Belgian carpenter came in to the camp again and tentatively agreed to my proposals about using his house. He wanted to meet me and to get assurance about my honourable treatment of his wife. I asked for plans of his village and house, methods of approach, etc. But after a lengthy pause he intimated that it was too big a risk and he would not have anything more to do with me.

Another set-back to my plans was the escape of ten Officers and men through a well-constructed, well-hidden tunnel, on a Saturday night in July. At *appel* the next morning it was noticed that men were missing and this naturally caused a stir in both camps. Muster followed muster. By 'walking' the potato field on the east side of the camp, the Germans discovered the outlet of the tunnel and by its position deduced that the inner end of it must be under Barrack 17 (the school) or Barrack 16. But, search as they would, it took them hours to find it, so cunningly had it been concealed under the steps at the southern end of Barrack 16. Captain Steel of the Port Line, was Barrack Captain at the time. In all we spent 7¼ hours on *appel* that day, and it was a Sunday I had chosen to remain in camp to do a few odd jobs, instead of going to the farmer for morning and midday meals.

The unexpected presence of guards, their officers and Gestapo in the camp on Sunday afternoon, had a surprising consequence. The 'farmers' had gone out in the morning before the escape had been detected and returned soon after 1.00 p.m. laden with the proceeds of a morning's trading. For the 'good' watch would be on the gate that day. The 'good' watch was on the gate all right, but backed up by Lieutenant Güsfeld who witnessed a most amazing haul of chickens, bread, cakes and eggs (a whole bath full). Seeing a fat bag about the neck of an American he put his hand in and – hey presto! – out came a live rabbit!

I was now apprehensive lest the Germans would confine us all to the camp. Closer supervision on the gate at least was to be expected and that would be a nuisance, if not a real danger to my taking equipment 'outside'. Some tightening up was, in fact, experienced and would have gone too far for my purposes if the Camp authorities had had their way. However, their scheme of having a soldier guard on the farms all day with each prisoner was quashed by opposition from the German farmers. So after a day or two we went out on the old terms; it was not long before 'trade' revived and we paid our entrance fee of a few cigarettes to the 'good' guard every third night and no questions asked.

The escapers had chosen a particularly bad patch of weather for their enterprise, or so it turned out. On the Saturday night a most violent thunderstorm with torrential rain, was experienced in the Elbe-Weser district and, to make it worse for those who had chosen to go to Bremen, a heavy night raid was under way on that city at the same time. Two of the fugitives were captured within a few hours, near the camp, having been found by a farmer. Within the next couple of days news of captures came in and rumours multiplied. I was naturally eager to glean every scrap of information about the venture, especially as regards equipment, difficulties the fugitives encountered and what led to their capture. Harry Gray was as helpful as possible in this connection. He was well placed for making contact with the re-captured men because he worked in Westertimke and sometimes managed to talk to them when they were out on the high road for their short daily exercise, as was the custom for men doing solitary confinement in the 'bunker'. Little of real value was learnt, however. More instructive was to see a youngster who had been re-captured about mid-week hauled back into the Lager. Poor dejected worn-out creature! Pale with exposure and exhaustion. How English he looked – no hat and a Burberry type of raincoat of a strikingly non-Continental cut.

The virtual failure of this mass escape gave me cause for serious reflection on the wisdom of jail breaking and, of course, it did nothing to inspire confidence. Furthermore, it was publicly announced that anyone found at large in civilian clothing would be treated as a spy and shot. But I did not take the unhappy incident as an excuse for changing my mind.

The unreliability of Bozo and Mico gave me some anxiety as to how the final details of the get-away could be arranged. Equipment and food had to be taken out of the camp piecemeal and secreted until *der tag*, and it had to be accessible at the last moment. There was scarcely a place in all the barns and outhouses safe from them or the farmer and his boys.

By happy chance my old shipmate Harry Harper, one of the few officer 'farmers', changed his job from Postles's farm to Blanken's farm which was also beside the church and close to Michaelis's. Secrecy had been so well kept that even this old friend of mine was unaware of my intentions. I now took him into my confidence and, in his characteristically generous manner, he took a very active part in my preparation and gave invaluable moral support and advice. Farmer Blanken was an old man and he left most of the work of running the farm to Harry, who had complete and unhindered access to all outbuildings, including an old house-cum-barn in which a strange hermit lived. This man had formerly lived in a turf cabin on the moor, but the war-time drive for man-power had compelled him to work in a small factory at Zeven and, presumably for convenience, he had taken up quarters in the old barn house. This was important to me in that amongst his few personal belongings he had an *Ausweis* (an identification certificate) which I was able to copy at my leisure. These barns, and a shed at the back of them, were a safe hiding place for my gear and a most convenient starting point for my adventure.

Smaller items of equipment were now acquired. German cigarettes '*Eckstein 5*' were obtained from French prisoners in exchange for English ones[1], and through them I also obtained Reich Marks. Two marks *Lager Geld* were exchanged for one R.M. (the French were able to send money home, paying in *Lager Geld*), and these transactions were usually made on Sunday mornings around the farm. The curiosity of Heinrich and Kallaheinz (the farmer's sons) was sometimes embarrassing. Harry did a splendid deal for me in acquiring a German peaked cap – rather a nautical uniform cap and very commonly used both in country and town by the working classes. This excellent article of disguise was bought from a widow for 100 English cigarettes. Her husband, its owner, had been killed on the Eastern Front. Smuggling things out of the camp presented no difficulty, in spite of the search at the gate. We were well accomplished in this art. The only real danger lay in being caught with an article or stores which would bring suspicion of escape upon oneself. Harry shared this work with me and, on nearing the farm, would take my stuff from me.

There were signs of improving weather and, by the time the rye was ready to cut, a hot spell had set in. This rye harvest was nearly my undoing, for Jan cut it with a grass mower and not a self binder, and so heavy was the labour of tying by hand these monstrous sheaves of six feet rye that I strained some muscles on my chest and

---

[1] *Although a non-smoker, I foresaw that cigarettes might be useful if I met people.*

simply had to remain at rest in the camp for some days. Before this accident had laid me up I was in a quandary. This was the weather I had been waiting for, but the work was so exhausting that the night's rest scarcely enabled me to recover my strength for the next morning. I was in no condition to make my escape effort. A substitute labourer was sent out in my place but was soon sent back again. In spite of his need, Jan Michaelis preferred to await my recovery than be humbugged by fellows whose last intention on going 'outside' was to work hard.

At this time, too, I was accustoming myself to sleeping out in the open. Knowing from experience of Scout camps how difficult it is to sleep out of doors the first night, I took to sleeping in a little bush surrounded hollow in our small garden, hard by Barrack 15, risking detection by the hounds that were brought into the camp at night. This went well for a time until one night I was awoken by a most terrifying roaring and droning. A thousand British bombers were hurtling through the dark sky on a terrible mission. They were going to destroy one of Europe's greatest cities – Hamburg. The eerie wail of sirens pulsed over the whole region as I stealthily gathered up my bedding and made a dash for the hut door, apprehensive now of the guards and their hounds. Inside, I quickly remade my bunk, turned in and lay listening. I was in a strange state of mind; there was a tinge of fear, a splash of exultation and a background of profound regret for what was happening. One could distinguish the difference in sound between the thunder of the defenders' cannonade and the deeper boom of the bombs which sometimes actually shook our hut.

The destruction of Hamburg really 'shook' the countryside. As the smoke pall drifted over a couple of days later, camp guards who had been on leave in Hamburg that weekend came back a few at a time, unshaven, blackened and burned, each with a nightmarish story of terror. Through them the local populace learned the ugly truth. The bombing of the Ruhr and other centres was well-known, but for the peasantry of Regierungs Bezirk Stade it had all been somewhat remote. This, however, was the *'krieg'* with a vengeance. The civilian driver of the weekend bus to Hamburg wasn't seen or heard of for days and his poor wife in Westertimke became nearly demented. Soon, evacuees began to arrive in our area by bus and lorry. I remember seeing a party of them, old and young, seated outside Willenbrock's Gasthof one day.

Although prisoners and foreign labourers were supposed to eat at separate tables, this rule was very seldom obeyed at Jan Michaelis's farm. Not only did we sit at table with the family, but with other Germans too, and when a pair of evacuee women from Bremerhaven were billeted in the house, we were even served with food before them.

Stephania and Mico lived in and were well treated. Herr Michaelis once told me how he and other farmers went to the neighbouring market town to get labourers. Each picked out the one he fancied from a pathetic group of males brought from the east. 'Just like buying an animal,' he said with honest disgust. Poor Mico, then a mere boy from the Ukraine, was almost wild. He even had to be taught how to use a knife and fork.

My return to health after the muscular strain unluckily coincided with a return of showery weather, so I began to think I might have missed my opportunity for this year. Nevertheless, my plan had matured and the project was as clearly conceived as it possibly could be in my state of knowledge. Captain Endreassen had ascertained from the Pastor of the Norwegian Seamen's Church in Hamburg, who visited Milag periodically to minister to his several compatriots, that Norwegian and Swedish merchant ships visited the ports of Hamburg and Harburg, but the contact could not say to what extent the recent bombardments had affected the operation of the ports themselves.

My room mate, Roland Hindmarsh, had acquired a black rubber mackintosh from one of the Dutch officers of KOTA NOPAN, and without asking awkward questions exchanged it for my own blue gaberdine. My photograph had come through from home – ostensibly that of my brother – and my pass was made out, though not finally completed because I had hoped for one with a more up to date format from the Royal Navy in Marlag, but they, in the end, failed me. So I had to be content with this copy of a temporary pass that was once issued to the hermit. I had no illusions about its real worth. However, it was something by way of identification. The photograph was genuine; and if produced with the requisite assurance and bluff about a temporary replacement of a lost document, my pass might fool a yokel in the *Landwacht*. The mere making of this Ausweis did at least bring me to decide upon my assumed identity. Bearing in mind a tip from Captain Von Rintelen[1], I kept my stated particulars as close to the truth as I could so as to minimize the risk of forgetting them. So my name Bird was given its German equivalent, Vogel, and so on. I was a carpenter from the Danish border (hence my accent) and for my domicile I couldn't resist using a place-name from that district, noticed when tracing my map – Wanderup.

By this time, too, it had become necessary to take 'Jock' Andrew, my 'combine' mate, into my confidence, because he was the storekeeper of our food. I would not take any of our stores without letting him know where they were going. Furthermore, he was to be entrusted with some of my personal belongings for safe keeping.

Arnt Ericson, a man from one of the 'Gothenburg ships', had been returned to Milag from Rendsburg jail[2] whence he had been transported with the Norwegians. Apparently his parents were of Swedish origin and he convinced the Germans that he was a Swedish citizen. They therefore saw fit to return him to Milag to await eventual release and repatriation to Sweden. I naturally visited him to enquire about my Norwegian friends and, at the same time, I took the chance of questioning him concerning shipping movements at Hamburg and in the Kiel Canal. As he rather carelessly talked about escaping – not believing in the German's promise to release him – I pumped him more than caution would normally permit. At this date, too, I was rather worried by my lack of exact knowledge of the manner and methods of ship search carried out by the Gestapo. Ericson had seen merchant ships moving through the Kiel Canal during his journey but had no concrete evidence. He rather alarmed me by remarking that he understood tear gas was employed by search parties for driving out stowaways. This news affected me so

---

[1] *The famous First World War spy and saboteur, who wrote 'The Dark Invader".*
[2] *This was the first confirmation that my friends had been kept in a German prison instead of being repatriated. It is sad to relate that before the end of the war about one third of those fine fellows had succumbed to starvation, illness, cold and brutal treatment in some of the worst German prisons and Concentration camps.*

much that I took steps to obtain a gas mask. But, having located a British civilian respirator in the camp, I decided that it was too bulky to include in my travelling kit. In any case, I had no means of determining whether it would be proof against tear gas, nor for how long.

My natural instinct in the science of meteorology was stimulated by a deeper study of it in the Camp school. There was plenty of time and opportunity for the observation of weather in our life on the farm and during those continual and often protracted stands in the open on *appel*. Fine weather was essential to my plan and my careful observation of weather sequences now enabled me to make fairly reliable forecasts, in spite of the lack of instruments.

On Sunday, 15th August, 1943, there were unmistakable signs of the approach of a fair period. On the Monday morning there was an occurrence which sent a strange thrill through me. Down in the shallow valley, blanketing the whole moor and pastures, lay a white fog gleaming in the early morning sunshine. In fact, it was the first fog I had seen while in Milag. I knew the time was at hand for the great decision, and Harry remarked quietly that the conditions were excellent for a 'break'. But it could not be that morning, for certain essential articles of escape were still in the camp. The day grew into one of those blazing August heats. We ate sour apples from the orchard to slake our thirst as we toiled in the barn unloading the seemingly endless procession of wagons of rye. The harvest was being gathered in. This was the time of fulfilment. Through me stole a feeling of inevitability. The die was cast. I would make the break tomorrow.

Back in the camp that night I took my usual bath, shaved carefully and cleaned my boots particularly well. The slit up the back of the raincoat had to be repaired and that took me nearly to 'lights out'. And so, with all the preparations completed, I went to bed and slept soundly.

Chapter Fourteen

Road to the Sea

On Tuesday morning, 17th August, I awoke and got up in good time. It was a lovely fresh morning, the dew sparkling on plants, trees and cobwebs in the early sunshine betokening a fine day. Once again a heavy mist lay in the valley. **The** day had dawned.

When dressed, I made the best use of my time in hurriedly breaking fast with eggs whipped up in 'KLIM', and I ate bread, butter and chocolate. Hermann, the guard, had made his last attempt to stir the laggards. The bell had clanked out its final warning for *appel*. All hands had left the room save myself and my friend 'Hoppie' (R. C. Hopkins) who, invariably late, was dragging a khaki pullover on to his tall thin body. This done in great haste, he ran his fingers through his fine dark hair, bracing himself for the frantic dash along the corridor 'Good-bye, Hoppie', I said, extending my hand. He took it automatically and before he could express his amazement at my gesture, I added, 'I am making a break today, going to try for a home run. Good-bye.' There was no time to say more. 'Good-bye, and good luck,' he said, warmly shaking my hand. Then he dashed away. I never saw him again.

Now entirely alone, I glanced around the old room festooned with odd garments, bedding still untidy, and my eyes rested fleetingly on my bunk in the corner, the centre of my little world for twenty months, the scene of some joys, many hopes and not a few despairs. It was in this moment that I became aware that I was in an unusual state of mind; not edgily anticipating all the difficulties before me but, despite my matter-of-fact, sceptical nature, completely at ease. It felt as if a pair of great hands was gently but firmly bearing me along. With no time to reflect on this, I picked up my precious German cap and hid it in my trousers, flung my mac over my arm, cloth side out to be less conspicuous, tapped my battle dress pocket to be sure my wallet was there, and set off briskly for the gate. Rigorous search was still the order of the day for the watch on the gate, and the sole duty of one soldier was to detect and brand any civilian clothing with KGF in bright red paint. Watching the gentleman carefully, I deliberately placed myself favourably in the ranks of the 'farmers' formed up three abreast ready to go out, and hung the mac on my arm as inconspicuously as possible. So, one at a time, we were frisked by the sergeant himself, then passed on to the clothing snooper. Knowing that unconcern and inconspicuousness were the key to success, I continued to gnaw away at my sandwich of black bread. I was in fact prepared with cloth for the removal of the paint from the rubber surface, a job which, I had concluded, could be done effectively. But this was not necessary, for the guard standing there with his paint pot, stencil and brush, completely overlooked me.

Soon we passed out of the inhospitable gates of Milag Nord, the column marching at its usual early morning dawdle in the silvery sunshine of that autumn day. The heavy labour of harvest was the lot of my companions this day. We stopped as usual after passing Lager Drei – the German quarters – and, turning to the grass verges, 'pumped ship'.

Forming up again, we marched on. The day promised well and, like a good omen, a heavy mist again lay on the low-lying land. Bozo, my Yugoslav comrade, had to be told of my intention, for he had certainly seen me in the 'gang' that morning, although I had tried to avoid his notice. Time was short. I went up the column, took him aside as safely as I could and tersely told him I was going to escape. If he was asked where I was, all he had to say was that he didn't know but supposed I had stayed in camp to see the doctor or dentist. (I had, in fact, made several feints of this nature, staying in the camp either with or without the farmer's knowledge, and going out on to the farm at lunchtime.) Finally I reminded him of the consequences of his wilfully giving me away.

We passed through the beautiful birch avenue leading us to the point where some of our party under one guard split off from the rest. My contingent continued up the main street under the two remaining guards and straggled along, out of formation, the prisoners just drifting off to their farms by the roadside as they came to them. The great moment was fast approaching; we were getting near the church. I could go to the right to Michaelis's farm, do my normal day's work and return to the shelter of Milag at night, or I could go left and in a few moments become a fugitive.

Our guards were more attentive to duty this morning; one walked ahead and the other followed in the rear of the column. That was not so good for my purpose as their more normal habit of chatting together, but we were all well strung out. So, with an anxious glance towards Michaelis's farm lest anyone had seen me, I took the way to the left over to Harry's farm. Harry came round the back of the barn with me. The sack containing my gear was taken from its hiding place in the lean-to shed and its contents were checked and found correct. I changed my khaki trousers for the dark brown corduroys and gave the former to Harry, for he would smuggle them back into the camp in case I was captured and should need approved leg covering. My things were quickly re-stowed in the sack. We rapidly applied Stockholm tar to the soles of my boots to destroy my scent in case of pursuit by hounds. I shook hands with my trusty friend. 'Good-bye, Harry!' 'Good-bye, Dickie, and good luck!' As I picked up the sack, I noticed a coil of wire to hand so took that also, thinking that if I were seen close to the village it would help to create the impression that I was off to the meadows to do a fencing job.

With sack on one shoulder and wire coil on the other, I walked as unconcernedly as possible over the dewy paddock to a gate in the further hedge. Beyond the hedge I looked up the village street. Good, the returning guards were not in sight. I hoped they would not be hanging about the back lane I was making for and wished to cross.

I noticed, but thought little of, my trail in the dew, guessing that it would soon vanish in the sunshine. Our calculation had been that my absence would not be detected until the gang returned to Milag just before eight o'clock in the evening. Even then, Harry would give my name instead of his own, so it would be nearly nine o'clock before the guards could possibly check who was actually missing by their method of visiting each 'farmer' in his barrack. That was a comforting thought. So, with a light heart and a springy step, I passed the odd outlying farm and the little carpenter's shop on the lane leading to the moor.

It was good to be abroad that morning, in bounding health, shod with a pair of well-greased and supple boots, and the way before me. There was not a soul to be seen. The milkmaids who were accustomed to milk their cows in the meadows bordering the lane, and whose curiosity I had feared, were not yet about.

After making this highly satisfactory progress for a quarter of a mile, I was struck by the fearful realization that I had left my German peaked cap behind in the shed; I had taken it from my trousers and had laid it down whilst changing, having previously decided to keep my customary beret on my head while in the neighbourhood of the village. A quick decision had to be made. The cap was my best piece of disguise. I would take the risk and go back for it. I hid my sack under a bush and returned to Herr Postles's farm, got my precious cap, re-tarred my boots and retraced my steps with a little less bounce in my gait. All went well and I carried on along the rough track to the peat moor. This was familiar ground and it was screened by bushes which fostered a sense of security. In a nicely secluded spot in the peat workings I emptied the sack, took off my battle-dress blouse, emptied the pockets and then donned a blue serge civilian jacket and the peaked cap. A sense of inner calm was very noticeable as I deliberately folded my discarded things and knelt to hide them under a bush. In that instant I felt surrounded by a mysterious yet benevolent presence. With humility uncharacteristic of my former attitude to life, I spontaneously said, 'Thy will be done;' and this strange experience stayed with me. I pocketed the wallet, slung the haversack over my shoulder, with the mac hanging from it and, filled with a sense of well being, strode off in the compass direction of the little township of Zeven.

My first objective was to get well away from the camp in case the hue and cry was raised earlier than anticipated, and to this end keeping to the moor and fields seemed the best course. The question as to whether one should travel by day or under cover of darkness had been discussed, but for lack of evidence I had decided to make judgement on the experience gained in these first few hours.

I came upon a tract of grassland divided into diminutive fields by shallow open ditches which had only the odd inch of water in them at this season. I took this further opportunity of destroying my scent by walking a good distance in the water before getting on to the bank again. My British Army boots, issued through the Red Cross, had been well greased many times and carefully used to make their stiff uppers pliable and waterproof, so I had no hesitation in paddling in that shallow water ditch. Inner soles cut out of Red Cross parcel cartons made them a good fit and promised reasonable foot comfort on the 50-mile march. A detail that caused me some misgiving was the brass eyelets. Brass was very scarce in Europe and no boots other than British ones had brass eyelets and after the original coat of black enamel had worn off them they shone conspicuously. How easy it is to overlook important details became alarmingly apparent within a few minutes. As I tramped on my course, it took me through a large area of tall, reedy, moorland grass. Waterproof the boots certainly were when sloshing through the shallow ditch water, but I had not foreseen their being swamped by the extraordinarily heavy dew on this grass which drenched my trousers and legs and gravitated into the boots from the top. To my consternation, the cardboard inner soles were reduced to pulp and my feet were sliding about in the boots, threatening sore feet in no time. I had failed to make and carry spare inner soles.

Soon there were other important matters to divert my mind from fretting over sore feet. Once across the moor, I encountered a hedge which bounded a partly ploughed field. The freshly furrowed land rose up from the flat moor and disappeared over a ridge to an invisible boundary beyond. The ploughshare had left the earth glistening in the morning sunshine, and to confirm the freshness of the work a pile of horse droppings at the headland was still steaming. How fortunate it is, I thought, that the keen awareness of their surroundings which is instinctive in wild creatures is quickly re-awakened in civilized man. After a short wait in hiding, I saw the horse-team, then the ploughman appear over the ridge. The horses' heads were nodding, their flanks sweating as they ploughed the easier down-hill furrow. Then round again on the laborious and slow up-run; with the ploughman's back to me, I had ample time to skirt round the field and get away. It seemed that playing hide and seek could still be fun for an adult. That little episode reminded me that constant vigilance was essential now I was out of the comparative safety of the moor.

The point was emphasized before the morning was out. Closer to Zeven, I noticed the edge of a quarry ahead, and my cautious approach to it was rewarded with a timely view of a gang of Russian prisoners down in the pit, working under armed guard. I watched the poor fellows for a while, then made an unhurried retreat and a detour of the quarry. This new course led to a field of rhubarb which was being harvested by a number of civilians and, unfortunately, necessitated my walking along an exposed railway in order to get past them. Suspecting that the bowed workers would stretch their backs from time to time and then catch eye of me, I strode along the track with an air of unconcern and confident step, all the time watching them from the corner of my left eye. Sure enough, a man stood erect and looked in my direction. He was about 250 yards away on my left. Instead of returning to his work, he began to walk up the field and converged on a rudimentary level crossing of the railway that I saw ahead. I noticed his bearing relative to my course, just as on a ship's bridge one would observe the bearing of another ship that was crossing. As we walked on, 'the bearing didn't appreciably change.' So, as the 'Rules for Prevention of Collision at Sea' tersely put it, 'risk of collision exists'. One cannot alter course on a railway. The best thing to do was to slow down a bit and let him cross the line well ahead of me. This stratagem seemed to be working out nicely. The man, a shortish fellow in grey civilian clothes, reached the level crossing while I was still a fair distance from him, and stepped on to the track. Oh hell! He stood their waiting for me. *'Guten morgen.'* *'Guten morgen,'* I replied in Platt Deutsch the lingua franca hereabouts. *'Woh gehen sie?'* (Where are you going?) he asked. Without hesitation I said, 'I am going home, I am a Danish carpenter. Unfortunately I have missed the train so I'm walking along the track. Where are you going?' 'Oh, I am going back to the lager. I don't think you should walk on the railway. Come to the lager with me.' Clearly it wasn't a good thing to stand there in the open arguing that point, in view of the other rhubarb pullers, although they were out of earshot. So I let him lead off to the right along a narrow path through a copse. As I followed, I undid my haversack so that the neck of my water bottle protruded and was handy to use as a weapon. The fellow, who turned out to be a Belgian, continued to chatter, although he had to walk in front through the thick bushes, and his questions were getting more and more pertinent. My right hand gripped the neck of the bottle. Should I cosh him? I didn't really want to harm him but . . . I was just deciding when we suddenly entered a small clearing and saw, walking towards us, a German army officer and his girl friend. I let the Belgian do the talking and, when near the German, interjected fairly loudly some *Ja's, Nein's* and *So's*. At that moment I was glad I had such a bona fide companion. Safely out of the copse, we walked along a field road towards the lager, a small encampment of foreign workers it seemed, situated close to a road and apparently without military supervision.

As we drew near, my mind was made up. 'I won't go into the lager,' I said. 'I'll carry on along the road,' and off I went. That stretch of road was straight and long and it seemed an age before I reached a bend where I could look back and see if anyone was in pursuit. To my relief the road was deserted.

The detour to the lager had upset my navigation, and until some recognizable place or signpost was encountered, it was a matter of heading in the right compass direction. Fortunately, the Germans, at this stage of the war, had not removed any of the normal road and town signs.

There was very little traffic on those country roads, a fact which cut both ways for a fugitive. For although one seldom met anyone, at each encounter one was exposed to the undistracted gaze of the other party. A vigilant look-out and timely evasive action seemed the best tactic. This was soon to be put to the test. I noticed a milk churn standing in the shade of a hedge. Cows had evidently been milked in the field that morning, for the churn was full and the cream had floated to the top, and the churn was awaiting collection. Without considering the question of ownership, I took a good swig of cream. Shortly, I saw two men coming on bicycles in the distance. They dismounted some distance up the road and went into a field off to the right, leaving their bikes by the roadside. At this stage I had come to the conclusion that travel by daylight was not unduly risky, and under the influence of my unseen 'helper' I felt the desire to press on. Within minutes I was examining the machines. Both were the familiar strong but hard-used farmers' bikes. A choice of two! The men were far away and I was well screened by a tall roadside hedge. What a gift! The tyres of the second machine could be deflated to hinder pursuit. Why, I could be in Harburg that night! It may be incredible that in response to an intuition I would not steal that bicycle, I felt I was not meant to do it, so left them there and marched on. Soon after befell a piece of good fortune. There, in mid-war Germany, meticulously scoured for every scrap of re-useable waste, was just what I needed lying by the roadside, a nice cardboard box from which I could renew the inner soles of my boots and relieve my feet.

That August afternoon the German countryside was sweltering under a blazing sun. When I got to the village of Sittensen I found the street deserted and shimmering in the oppressive heat. It was a very long street and I marched along on the right-hand pavement, all alone on that hot day. I thought I must look conspicuous with a black rubber mac dangling from my haversack. Suddenly, to my horror, there appeared far down that very long street, on the opposite side of the road, a uniformed policeman, coming towards me. To turn back would invite suspicion. There seemed no escape from an encounter, so I marched on with apparent confidence and unconcern. The policeman was wheeling a bicycle and talking to a woman walking on the pavement beside him. It seemed an age before they got near. The policeman continued to talk with his head turned toward the woman. Any moment he might look left, come over and officiously bark out a challenge. My self-confidence did not desert me. I didn't look at the officer, though in fact I was as sensitive as a wild animal to his every movement and gesture. Was it fate? Neither the policeman nor the woman looked at me. I seemed to be invisible to them. I felt as if I had taken part in a miracle.

I am naturally inclined to perspire freely and need plenty to drink. On that sultry day it posed a problem when I emptied my water bottle. Eventually I came to a market garden, and without the least trepidation went and asked permission to fill my bottle. This was done without any questions being asked, and again I tramped eastward along the straight, birch-tree lined roads of the Luneberg Heide, till the shadows lengthened in front of me.

By nightfall I found myself near a piece of woodland and decided to explore the possibility of spending the night there. The trees were not dense; there was plenty of heather on the sandy soil beneath them and scattered bushes created an air of seclusion. A small, placid stream ran nearby. It seemed an ideal spot. The weather was dry and settled. First I had a frugal meal. Next I made a nice springy bed of heather and spread the mac on it, and after a quick wash at the stream I thankfully laid down fully clothed, pulled the mac around me and, before putting my head down on my haversack, drew heather as best I could over my body. I gazed up into the clear sky. The fir tree tops were silhouetted in the pale light of the rising moon. The night was calm, its stillness disturbed only by the low rumble of traffic on the distant *autobahn*. What a day to look back on!

The most amazing feature of it was the unexpected and unaccountable feeling of a providential power within and around me. It evaporated fear, yet it prompted me to be keenly sensitive to all about me and to exercise all possible caution. With a thankful heart my tired frame lapsed into sleep.

During the night I awoke shivering. My whole body shook violently, my teeth chattered and it was alarming to find I had no control over these convulsions. For a while I lay in this state looking at the full moon, now high in the clear sky. This trouble had not occurred when I had slept out in the camp, so in these good conditions it was an inexplicable and a very disturbing experience. If this continued, I reflected, it would wreck my chance of success. I felt I couldn't stand many nights like this. Perhaps a bit of exercise would help. In fact it did. A few 'jerks' stimulated the blood circulation, the quaking subsided and, after remaking the bed, I put my head down again and got some fitful sleep before dawn.

Fortunately, and surprisingly, the experience did not exhaust me. Toilet by the stream, including a shave, refreshed me. While thus engaged I heard a strange sound coming intermittently from high up in the trees. This excited my curiosity so much that I cautiously went closer to the source of the sound. Soon I was rewarded by the sight of a strange bird. Black and white, with a red cap, obviously a kind of woodpecker, it was creeping up a high branch and every now and again pecking at the bark, making a loud drumming noise. My elation of the previous day returned. Perhaps because I was a fugitive and of necessity living close to nature, I felt an affinity with wild things, and humility and gratitude. Then I put reverie aside. I had to get on. Fortified with a breakfast of Canadian biscuits, with butter and Yeastvite, I was soon ready for the road.

It was with an almost jaunty air that I set off on my second day of freedom. Loneliness was not a burden. On the contrary, it was a pleasure after two years of captivity in the over-crowded conditions of the Raider and the Camp to have a bit of solitude, excellent though my fellow prisoners were. Rational discussion of the situation and all the potential hazards with a companion would, I felt, probably cause the mystical dimension to evaporate. I felt at ease. As nearly all the crops had been harvested, the fields and the country roads were deserted, except for the farm wagon coming round the bend ahead. The farmer was sitting up on the empty wagon. The horse, one of the lighter breed used in those parts, ambled along at a smart walking pace. A greeting was unavoidable so, wishing to have the initiative, I spoke first in Platt. 'Are you carrying corn today?' The farmer, reining in his horses as if intent on having a chat, asked 'Where are you going?' A little surprised by my own boldness and intending not to risk a conversation, I kept walking but turned and replied, '*Nach hause*' (I'm going home). I heard the farmer urge his horse to start but would not look behind to see if I was being pursued. The crunch of iron wheels on the road metal grew fainter. Once round the bend, I hopped over the hedge and waited a while in the field, half expecting the farmer would think it his duty to investigate this stranger or alert the police. Fortunately, it seemed he did neither.

The intense heat once more gave rise to the problem of replenishing my water bottle. No river or stream was to be seen and most of the ditches were dry. At length I found one in which there was a little running water and filled up the bottle. I put it to my lips to drink. The water was contaminated by sewage, although there was no habitation in sight. Cursing, I spat it out. Eventually the road led me near an old farm house with a thatched roof. In front was a well with a windlass. It seemed safer to ask for water rather than be forced into an awkward explanation if I were caught drawing it without permission. So I knocked on the door. After what seemed a long delay it was opened by an old crone who apparently could not understand my simple request. In fact, she seemed to be deaf. Apprehensive lest she should go to fetch someone else, I pointed to my bottle and then the well. She understood and went indoors. The well was remarkably deep. It seemed an eternity before the bucket reached the water and a correspondingly long interval before the clanking chain on the squeaky windlass hove the full bucket to the surface. The bottle was quickly rinsed out, my thirst quenched and the bottle refilled.

At ease again, I marched on and the rhythm of my feet awakened tunes and songs of brisk tempo. 'Keep right on to the end of the road' was persistent, and inspiring too. There were pleasant intervals when my thoughts wandered into all sorts of by-ways. When resting in a ditch, I remembered a story of Winston Churchill's escape from the Boers, and recalled a picture of him in hiding in a similar shelter – though with a vulture perched nearby anticipating a meal. I was glad I was spared the vulture. My attention was attracted by something on the bare earth of a newly ploughed field – silvery strips. I picked some up. They were about nine inches long and half an inch wide, aluminium foil on one side, black paper on the other. I had heard of such radar baffling devices. In an indefinable way they gave me encouragement. I handled them fondly. They must have been in Britain a day or so ago. At that moment home seemed not so far away.

Towards evening the landscape mellowed. The dour stubble fields had given place to softer meadows and I was just thinking how English the scene was when a thrilling sound came to my ears. It was a ship's whistle. I took that to be a good omen. A quick glance at the map confirmed that my pleasant country road would soon join the main approach road to the port from the north west. Not long afterwards, I had the satisfaction of seeing an artistic sign standing on the grass verge, bearing a coat of arms and informing the traveller that he was entering the district of Harburg.

Luckily, the euphoria of this happy ending to a successful day had not dulled my sensitivity to danger. On the main road entering the suburbs I spotted a road block and police checkpoint in ample time to evade it. This I did by simply climbing up the steep, tree-covered bank running along the right hand side of the road and walking along it in the cover of the trees until the checkpoint was past. Soon there were villas to be seen on that side, standing in extensive grounds on the same higher level. Night was falling, so it was opportune to find a resting place. The grounds were not the trim, well-groomed gardens found in Britain, but rather enclosures of natural heath, slightly modified to produce a nice visual effect. This was fortunate, for it meant there was no difficulty in finding a heathery spot for a bed, well away from houses and with easy access to the road.

Catering for supper didn't present any difficulty, nor take much time. I was glad to remove my boots and lie down and relax on my heather bed. It had been a fine day's march. Physically I was in good trim, feet included, in spite of low rations and the hot weather. I was in excellent spirits and quietly hopeful that now the unplannable phase of the adventure had been reached, the way ahead would be revealed. I sank down into the heather, thankful for my strange lot. Within minutes I fell fast asleep.

CHAPTER FIFTEEN

The Kap Horn

Fortunately, the ague-like condition of the previous night did not recur. The immediate problem on my early waking was how to get a satisfactory shave and wash without using too much drinking water from the bottle. Yesterday, at the river, there had been no such difficulty. Now, the outcome was a good shave but barely enough water left to help down the dry Canadian biscuits. I reckoned that my rations would last two more days and that, as planned, I could starve for two more without undue distress.

It was imperative to leave my 'hotel' before the neighbours were astir, and that suited me, for I was keen to get into the town and discover the lay-out of the docks and take a peep at the bridge over the Elbe to Hamburg. The bright, sunny morning bred optimism and that mood was greatly excited by a glimpse of the river and a cargo ship flying the Dutch flag. So, sea-going ships were using Harburg; that was most encouraging!

As I tramped along the pavement beside the main road leading into town, I had not forgotten the need of water, nor the increasing difficulty of re-filling the bottle in a built-up area; but I felt no undue concern. The immediate problem was solved in a flash. A short distance ahead, a man, who looked a professional type, was getting into his motor car and a woman in servant's dress was rendering some kind of assistance. The car drove away and, as I approached, the maid disappeared through the side door of a house. I immediately went up the steps and rang the bell, and in a moment a pleasant young woman in uniform opened the door. Smiling cheerfully, I asked if I could have some water and held out my bottle. Off she went and filled it. I thanked her and wished her good morning. After two years of exclusively male company it was pretty good to get a smile from an attractive girl. A door plate indicated that this place was a dental surgery.

Accommodation in an hotel never entered into my plans, for

several reasons. Although no problem would arise until evening, I was prompted, when passing a vacant plot big enough for three houses, to step off the pavement into the bushes to investigate the site. It was ideal. There was no roadside fence so, on approach, one could just go into the wild bushes and disappear. Conversely, when wishing to emerge, one could view the pavement and road from cover and only step out when it was clearly safe to do so. Through the bushes at the back of the site were several trees – the largest one being an oak with a trunk about fifteen inches in diameter. It stood on the bank of a dry ditch. Beyond that ditch was another much deeper and broader ditch with water and reeds in it; and on the other side of that was a double-track railway with allotment gardens beyond. At one side of the plot was the back of the little Hotel zum Forsthaus that fronted on to a side lane that crossed the railway. On the other side was an air-raid shelter and a Hitler Youth hut. On the opposite side of the road was a tree-covered embankment. What a Godsend! Without more ado, I metaphorically checked in to the 'room' in the dry ditch beneath the friendly oak. I took off my conspicuous haversack and mac and hid them under a bush.

With a yet lighter step I started a reconnaissance of the town. There was but little evidence of bomb damage, in spite of its proximity to Hamburg, 'blitzed' a few weeks before. I had no detailed map of the town and, as I had not visited the port (as I had Hamburg on several occasions) before the war, I decided to reconnoitre. One look at the great Elbe bridge was enough to confirm that the policemen stationed there checked the papers of everyone wanting to cross into Hamburg. So, before risking police scrutiny on the way to the larger seaport, the first task was to find out what chances Harburg appeared to offer. Several empty quays were visible from the public way, but the Dutch ship was nowhere to be seen and that indicated that there were other wharves in the port and, maybe, other ships. As I had anticipated, the best tactic seemed to be to make contact with foreign sailors to glean a few salient facts about guards on the docks and ships, passes carried by ships' crews and, not least, the whereabouts of ships, if any, going to Sweden or, at a pinch, Norway. A sailor knew, almost by instinct, where to find a pub or two strategically sited around the docks. I soon located one and it had the encouraging name of 'Kap Horn'. Satisfied that I could not do more at the moment, I returned to the ditch to have a little to eat and to rest, preparatory to going back to the pub in the evening.

In the leafy seclusion of my new abode I reviewed my prospects for this new phase of the adventure. I had a number of advantages. Familiarity with docks, ships and the ways of seafarers were high on the list. Though my command of the German language was not great, my months on the farm had given me confidence that I could understand anything of importance and deal with everyday situations. I had studied Swedish before the war, and in the camp I had become fairly proficient in Norwegian; it seemed to me those languages might prove to be useful. I had noticed foreign workers about the town and concluded that I was much less conspicuous than most of them. My clothing, dissociated from the haversack, was quite satisfactory. A nautical touch could now be given to my peaked cap for use around the docks. I took out my shipping company's cap badge and attached it to my cap with a large safety pin that I had acquired for the purpose. It was another remarkable coincidence that Trinder, Anderson's badge contained within the usual golden laurel wreath a bright blue enamelled flag with a yellow cross in it – the Swedish flag! It was of little account that there was a tiny Australian black swan in the middle of the yellow cross. There were things on the minus side too, but I had no inclination to contemplate my diminutive stock of food or think about the short time available to accomplish my purpose. That would be an affront to my mystical helper. 'Sufficient unto the day . . .' When I was preparing for my evening in town, I made a somewhat disquieting discovery. Under the bush where I had chosen to make my bed I found the nose of an ack-ack shell. That made me ponder the old saying that lightning never strikes twice in the same spot; and hope it was true of shell splinters.

At length I made my way back to the Kap Horn. It was empty. I ordered a beer and sat down and quietly sipped it, seemingly at ease. Before long, four men came in and sat down to drink at a nearby table. They looked like seafarers. They spoke in rather low tones, so I could not catch what language they used. Almost certainly it was not German and there was nothing about the men to suggest that they were Dutch. They began to light cigarettes and I thought I saw a little picture, a simple outline sketch of a baby, on one side of an otherwise commonplace matchbox. That momentary glimpse sent a thrill of excitement through me, for I knew that in Sweden such boxes of matches were sold at a fractionally higher price than normal, the little extra going to a children's charity. Those matches must have been bought in Sweden and the men must have been there recently. I took out my own cigarettes and went over to beg a light, speaking in German. Yes, for sure, they were **Solstickorna**. On handing the box back I casually asked, in Swedish, 'Are you Swedish?' To my surprise, this civil question provoked a very curt and rough, 'No we are not,' for an answer. I thanked them and then retired to my own table to smoke my cigarette and ponder the situation. The four departed, leaving me slightly bewildered and not inclined to follow them. No other likely customers came in before I deemed it time to return to the ditch for a night's rest. Although I had not been able to take a positive step in the direction of freedom on this first day in Harburg, I felt a glow of satisfaction and thankfulness for the day's work. I had tested my nerve in calling at a town house for water; the Dutch boat proved that foreign vessels were using Harburg and the **Solsticka** matches showed that in all probability a vessel that had been to Sweden was in the port. Those reflections were a good nightcap and I slept well on them.

First thing next morning I began my toilet. I regarded it as essential to maintain a well-shaven and washed appearance and had brought the necessary equipment for that purpose with me. Well, not quite what I needed. There was water enough in the deepish, steep-sided, wet ditch but, apart from my bottle, I had no means of obtaining any of it. And, now knowing the quality of that water, I was hesitant to risk contaminating the little I had by using the bottle. It was at that moment that I had another amazing practical demonstration of providential assistance. There, in the dry ditch, though I hadn't seen it before, was a white enamelled mug. Inside it was a mixture of paints of several colours. But they were water-bound paints, which washed out easily to reveal a perfectly good and unchipped mug. With a spare bootlace tied on the handle I could easily draw all the water I needed.

It was not long after this stroke of good fortune that it seemed as if the whole adventure would collapse. Without warning I came over light-headed and was getting delirious. Fancy having to stagger out on to the road and give myself up! Yet if this illness continued, or got worse, that would be better than passing out in the ditch. I realized I was on a low diet but I hadn't felt unduly hungry and certainly not weak. I still had a full day's rations in my bag, so I decided to eat a Canadian biscuit with Yeastvite on it. Then I remembered the small tin of Yeastvite was empty. It was one of those small round flattish tins with a press-on lid. There might be a little Yeastvite left round the inner side of the lid opening. I ran the tip of my little finger round the inside of the tin and, sure enough, found a smear of Yeastvite there, in all about the size of a pea. I sucked this off my finger. It was good! Why did I relish it so much? Why did it taste so good? In an instant the answer came to me. Salt! I remembered reading Julian Huxley's essay on the salt/water ratio in the human body. That was it. I had been drinking a lot, and sweating profusely, yet taking in but little food with an adequate amount of salt in it. It was do or die, so without hesitation I went to a little general store I had seen down the road the previous day and bought some salt. There were tomatoes on sale too, so I bought half a kilo of them and went back to the ditch and ate them, liberally sprinkled with the salt. In about half an hour I felt quite well again. I had also discovered that small salted fish about the size of sardines could be bought without a ration card. So, when I recovered, I went back and joined the queue for them. Queuing had never been my favourite pastime but in these circumstances it was invaluable. Long before it was my turn to be served I heard the name of the fish repeated many times and got a good idea of how much to ask for. One might provoke unwelcome attention by asking for either a silly little quantity or a ridiculously large amount. The price per hekto was shown on a ticket. Those fish went down well with Canadian biscuits.

There was no sign of a seafarer in the Kap Horn or the neighbourhood of the dock that evening. I returned to the ditch, not noticeably disappointed by the apparent waste of a precious day. This was odd, considering it was the end of the fourth day out and the larder was nearly empty. Perhaps the new-found source of food helped to keep up my spirits.

Before I turned in I had a strident reminder that the war was still on. The chilling wail of air-raid sirens was quickly followed by the cacophony of flak. I remembered the shell nose cap I had found a couple of feet away from where I was now sitting with my back to the oak tree. As the raid got hotter and noisier, I was trying to weigh up the risks of going into the local public air-raid shelter against the danger of remaining in the open. Before I had decided what to do a yet more urgent situation arose. Someone was coming towards me through the bushes. The intruder moved right up to the oak tree and sat down. There we were – the stranger atop the bank with his back to the oak, I in the ditch with my back to the other side of the tree. How long the raid lasted I couldn't guess. It seemed a long time to be absolutely motionless and fearful of an involuntary sneeze or cough. Eventually the racket diminished, then ceased. Was there movement on the bank? Very, very cautiously I inched round to see. The man had gone! Perhaps he was a homeless fugitive too! I thought those R.A.F. fellows were quite considerate of my interests to get their raid over before one o'clock so I could get a little sleep that night.

It was now Saturday. Time was running out and I wondered whether I should stick to the passive tactic of waiting to meet foreign seafarers in the hope of obtaining information or take a more active course. Should I try a more daring daylight reconnaissance of the docks to see how I might board a likely craft at night to stow away? I am by nature an 'activist' and if tactics had to be decided by discussion with a fellow escaper there is no doubt how my vote would have been cast. As it was, my 'companion' didn't argue the pros and cons but in a strange way intimated the right course. So I spent the day quietly in and near my 'hotel', attending to my toilet (shaving soap running out) and shopping for more fish and tomatoes to eke out the few remaining Canadian biscuits.

In the evening I went to the Kap Horn to continue my vigil and whiled away the time drinking beer. It was getting late before anyone of interest appeared. This pub was the last port of call for sailors returning from town to their ships. Suddenly the drowsy bar was animated by the arrival of four men in high spirits. They were seafarers but not Germans. When they were seated and had got their drinks, I took out a cigarette and, pretending I was short of a match, went over and begged a light. They were Dutchmen. I got into conversation with them. I tried to tell them in German that I was a Norwegian sailor. I had been ashore with the girls, had been robbed of most of my possessions and missed my ship. Now I was trying to get home. This was a situation that immediately aroused the sympathy of fellow seamen of an occupied country. One man quickly told me, in Norwegian, that he had been on a ship trapped in one of the Fjords earlier in the war and, during an enforced stay of five months, had learnt a good deal of the language from a Norwegian girl friend. Fortunately I had a much greater command of Norwegian than the Dutchman, but from now on we two conducted a conversation in that language. A highly interesting situation arose when the Dutchman was stuck for a Norwegian word. He referred to the bo'sun in Dutch. The bo'sun would tell me the English equivalent of the missing word and I, having admitted to knowing a little English, would indicate that I understood, and then the conversation would be resumed in Norwegian. Whilst I thoroughly enjoyed the amusing aspect of the occasion, I was even more pleased by the information my new friend was conveying in broken Norwegian. The Dutch ship had brought iron ore from Sweden, she was still discharging it and was most likely returning for more. There were no personnel checks at dock entrances but ships' gangways were guarded by uniformed Germans. The Gestapo searched ships before they sailed. I raised the question of my getting a passage to Sweden. My story of the Norwegian sailor had been taken so completely at its face value that the Dutchmen supposed I wished to sign on as a member of the crew. And they went to some length to explain that there were no vacant berths. By this time it was rather late and the Dutchmen indicated that they wanted to go aboard. I left Kap Horn with them with the intention of pressing the matter of a passage and finding where their ship was berthed. As we stumbled along the railway in the docks in the blackout, I put out feelers about stowing away on my own initiative, but the Dutchmen didn't respond favourably. They didn't know when they would sail, the Gestapo search and other hazards were given as reasons for not embarking on that course. As my initial hopes of obtaining active assistance from these men were fading and I was beginning to think that the only remaining benefit that I might yet get out of the situation was to discover the ship's whereabouts, a dramatic change took place. The black bulk of a ship's stern loomed up out of the darkness. Then we had to make a detour round the end of a gangway. The shadowy figures of the watchmen emerged from the warmth of the ship's galley, but quickly returned when they saw the rather noisy party was not boarding their ship. As we walked the length of the ship I pursued my suggestion of stowing away on the Dutchman. After all, I reasoned, I had to get out of Germany somehow and, having missed my ship and lost my papers, I didn't care to give myself up to the German authorities. We had reached the bows of the ship. The bo'sun stopped and called out loudly in English 'Ahoy there!'. A dim figure leaned over the rails above them. 'We have a Norwegian sailor here who has missed his ship, will you help him?' 'O.K.' was the quick response and within seconds a ladder was lowered on to the quay. I said goodbye to the Dutchmen and rapidly ascended the ladder and followed my helper down below into the fo'c's'le. In the blinding light of the sailors' messroom I saw the four men who had curtly told me in the Kap Horn that they were not Swedes. It was quickly apparent why. They were Danes, and in their country's wretched state of occupation by the Germans they were not well disposed towards the Swedes who had managed to keep out of the war. I re-told the stranded-Norwegian-sailor tale. I spoke in Norwegian, knowing that written Danish was almost identical, but that the pronunciation of Danish was so very different that Norwegians, unaccustomed to hearing the other language, can only with difficulty understand it. The same applied to Danes hearing Norwegian; so any shortcomings in my Norwegian might pass unnoticed. My story was not questioned, nor was I challenged in any way. These boys just reacted splendidly to a fellow sailor in distress. First, they gave me food and plenty of it, and some good hot *'ersatz'* coffee to wash it down. There was no need to simulate hunger. The friendly Danes answered all my questions about their ship. Yes, she had brought iron ore from Sweden via the Kiel Canal. They expected to return to Sweden when unloaded, but not Norway, though the latter was not impossible. I said I would very much like to go with them, even if it meant stowing away. The mention of stowing away prompted the Danes to tell a doleful story of two Frenchmen who had stowed away on a previous trip. They had hidden themselves under the coal in one of the bunkers. The Gestapo, furnished with long iron bars and Alsatian police dogs, had sniffed and probed them out, mishandling them in a dreadful fashion. So they would not advise stowing away. But, when they perceived that I was not deterred by the Frenchmen's bad luck, they said, surprisingly, that I had better come aboard next morning and speak to the Captain, adding that he was a 'Mission's man'. The latter remark was rather more surprising than that they referred me to the Skipper. Before I left, these generous fellows packed up a good parcel of bread, marge, cheese and meat to take away. I left by the unofficial gangway, noted well the position of the ship, then with a light step made my way back to the ditch. I was thankful for a very profitable day and was much encouraged by the ability to go in and out of the dock area unchallenged. The heavy thunderstorm with torrential rain that broke in the middle of the night didn't dampen my spirits.

A Daring Encounter

Sunday morning dawned, the storm had passed and I found that I had managed to keep fairly dry and even get some sleep. After a real breakfast and a shave, I set out for the docks and found the little Danish vessel. A German watchman stood at the top of the gangway. I went up without hesitation and in my most commanding German barked out 'Where is the Captain?' It worked. Without question, the watchman directed me to the saloon. The Skipper's cabin was off the saloon, the door was open and he was inside listening to a church service from Denmark on the radio. Speaking in Norwegian, I asked to be excused for interrupting the Captain's listening and then spun him the stranded-Norwegian-sailor yarn. The look in the Captain's eyes encouraged me to say I hoped I could stow away just before the ship sailed and do it so that neither the Captain nor crew would be incriminated. The Captain repeated the story of the two unfortunate Frenchmen and emphasised that he thought any stowaway on board was bound to be detected. Though he was obviously sympathetic, I saw that I had got to make a much stronger appeal to him, so I shut the door and turned to him and said in English, 'Captain, I'm a British Merchant Navy Officer, I have escaped from a prison camp and want to get to Sweden, can you help me? His reaction was very warm. I said I was confident I could make a pre-planned stowaway without incriminating him or his crew if I were found. On the spur of the moment I indicated the locker space under the seating around three sides of the saloon tables as a possibility. 'Why, the Germans would sit there to have a drink and that would be the last place they would look for a stowaway,' I said. The Captain replied, 'We are winning the war. It will soon be over. Don't take the risk. Go back to your Camp. You'll only be caught if you do stow away.' He was so obviously sincere and well-meaning that I had to accept his gentle refusal to co-operate. This was indeed a tantalizing situation. Before a cordial farewell the Captain produced a stick of shaving soap for me. I had no intention of taking the Skipper's bad advice about returning to Milag. Indeed, the idea of it made me laugh, nor did I feel depressed by this apparent failure. After all, I had gained some extremely valuable information and experience within the last few hours, which gave me confidence that in time I would succeed – if only I could keep alive. At the moment it looked as if I could last until Tuesday. But there was no luck for me at the Kap Horn that night either.

Next day, Monday, I made for the docks in daylight and a wonderful sight met my eyes. A big Swedish ship was discharging iron ore at a hitherto deserted jetty. When I had taken in this exciting scene, I realized there was one big snag. The ship was lying at the far end of the long jetty which was totally exposed to view and had only one way on and off it. To approach the ship in daylight on a work day without an adequate excuse if challenged, was not a sensible thing to do. I was hesitant to try at night without further information so, once again, I spent the evening in and around the Kap Horn, but there was no sign of a Swede nor any other foreign seaman.

On the Tuesday afternoon I went to look longingly at the ship. To my surprise and delight, there was another Swedish ship, a small one called 'POLE STAR', tied up at the landward end of the jetty. It seemed too good to be true. So, with Trinder, Anderson's Swedish-looking cap badge firmly pinned to my peaked cap, I determined to board her right away in daylight. The tide had ebbed and the little ship's deck was well below the quay. An ordinary ladder was being used as a gangway. There were two uniformed Germans on the deck at the bottom. As I swung onto the ladder and started to descend, one of them called out in German, 'What do you want?' I stopped and replied, 'To visit my friends in the crew.' The Germans asked 'Forward or aft?' and seemed satisfied when I said 'Forward' (i.e. the sailors' not the officers' quarters). I resumed the descent. When halfway down, I was again challenged. 'Where have you come from?' I pointed to the big Swede. 'Have you got your pass?' With an instant reaction, triggered off by some deep instinct of self-preservation, I felt my breast pocket. 'Oh no, I haven't. I left it aboard.' The German said, 'I think you had better to back and get your pass.' I agreed and climbed up the ladder and out of the tricky situation. Having said that I came from the big Swede, I knew it was prudent to walk towards her while in sight of the Germans. As I got closer to her fine flared bows and was wondering what the next move should be, a man dressed in a red shirt spat into the dock and hissed out some very rude words to the effect that he was not a Nazi. Thereupon I said, 'I am a British Merchant Navy seaman escaped from a prison camp, can you help me to get out of Germany?' With no more display of surprise or emotion than you would expect if the request had been for a match, the sturdy, dependable-looking Swede nodded assent but said, 'It's too early and too light. Do you know the Kap Horn? You will find three of my shipmates there; they will help you. I am going to visit friends on POLE STAR.' I didn't doubt his word for an instant, though obviously he could have said what he did to get rid quietly of an awkward customer. As we walked along the quay, I mentioned my attempt to board POLE STAR and asked the Swede to tell the Germans, if necessary, that I also was a member of his crew. We parted in view of the German watchmen.

CHAPTER SIXTEEN

Stowaway

The bar of the Kap Horn was empty when I got there but I felt no concern about that. Rather than wait indoors I patrolled the deserted dock road, knowing that any crew returning to LUOSSA – for that was the ship's name – must pass that way. Presently two figures appeared in the distance, and when they drew near it was plain that they were Swedish sailors. One even wore a bobble hat of wool in the national colours, blue and yellow. I accosted them and, speaking Swedish, bluntly asked if they were Nazis. Their reply was as emphatic as their shipmate's earlier. Then I told them of my meeting with the man in the red shirt. 'Oh yes,' said the elder, 'that would be Motorman Anderson.' Their reaction to my request for help was instantaneous and splendid. 'Of course we will help you, but it's still too early. We must wait till it's dark. Let's go back into the town for a while to have a drink and talk it over. My name is Erick Solberg, AB., and this is Edvin Nielson, O.S.' The Golden Hind was a livelier pub than the Kap Horn they said. It was full of people drinking and singing; sailors, civilians and many soldiers on leave. We found a table near the door at which their shipmate, Motorman Henry Wendt, was sitting. We ordered beer and joined in the choruses. I was anxious to assure my new friends, Erik, Edvin and Henry, of my bona fides. I was glad to be able to tell them of my long-standing friendship with the then famous Swedish journalist, Alf Martin, *later awarded the O.B.E.*, London Correspondent of the *Göteborgs Handels & Sjöfarts Tidning*, and now radio commentator and interpreter of the British scene to the Swedes. I mentioned my two visits to their country and my genuine admiration for their life-style and the way they conducted their affairs. After a week on the run, with everyone about me a potential enemy, it was exhilarating to be able to talk freely to these warm-hearted fellows who accepted me as a brother. Plans were made for getting aboard and, when darkness fell, we quietly slipped out of the Golden Hind and made our way to

LUOSSA. On nearing the ship, Edvin went aboard at the gangway, at the far end and engaged the German watchmen in conversation. His job was to enthuse about the German girls he had met and generally chatter, to hold their attention. Henry followed him after a minute or so. When he had checked that the two Germans were still at the head of the gangway and nicely engaged by Edvin, he walked forward on the main deck as far as the bridge and then gave a low whistle to indicate that all was clear. At this signal Erik began stumbling along the quay singing a bit, pretending to be slightly drunk. My task was to board the ship abreast of the foremast under cover of Erik's diversion. I cautiously moved from the shadow of a crane towards the ship's side. The Devil! We had all forgotten to take the tide and loading into account. The ship was floating so high that I couldn't reach the plating below the railing. There was only one way to get on that deck and that was to make a jump and hope to grab the lowest rail. There was a big German-type bollard on the quay to which a back spring of the mooring was made fast. That would give me a three feet start if I could jump from the top of it. Unfortunately, the ship's side was a couple of feet away from the quay at the position of the bollard. I quickly sized up the situation. I would have to risk falling in the dock, so before attempting the leap I took the precaution of discovering where the nearest ladder was in the quay wall. It wasn't far away. With my trusty boots and haversack slung round my neck, I got on to the bollard and sprang upward as high as I could and luckily grabbed the lower rail silhouetted against the night sky. Silently I hauled myself up and over the rail. In stockinged feet I began crossing the deck towards No. 2 hatch. Suddenly a match was struck on the lower bridge which, in the black-out, seemed to illuminate the whole ship. In a flash I realized that whoever lit his cigarette would be momentarily blinded, so like lightening I bounded over the deck and tumbled down the booby hatch near the mast and stood panting in the 'tween deck. I was thankful I was familiar with ships; a landsman in that darkness might have gone headlong to his death down in the lower hold. As arranged, I made my way cautiously along the 'tween deck till I came to a bulkhead at the after end of the ship. There was a door and Erik was waiting for me. We went further aft to a small steel-plated room which housed a

M.S. LUOSSA

central heating boiler, not in use at this season. This is where I would sleep tonight. The boys soon brought me some excellent Swedish food, and with many apologies for my having to sleep on the bare steel deck, wished me a very good night. And a very good night it was. A feather bed would not have felt more comfortable than that good solid steel deck of a Swedish ship sailing for Sweden the next day. I felt overwhelmingly grateful to the Providence that had brought me safely to this lodging and I slept soundly.

Early next morning, Erik came to the boiler room with food and coffee for breakfast. He said the iron ore cargo would all be discharged before noon and the ship would sail down the Elbe and anchor off Brunsbüttel at the entrance to the Kiel Canal that night. He didn't expect the German authorities to conduct a search of the vessel before it left Harburg; that was usually done at Kiel but, as a precaution against a sudden change in routine, the boys intended to hide me under a pile of dunnage wood in the 'tween deck. I didn't find the long wait boring. On the contrary, it was a great pleasure to hear real shipboard sounds after twenty months in the prison camp, and to sit there and visualize what was going on. Eventually the boys came and conducted me along the 'tween deck. German stevedores on the deck above were putting on the beams and hatch boards ready for battening down. Anyone who did not see this little party making its way along the 'tween deck didn't guess its purpose. At a spot out of sight of the Germans covering the hatches, I dirtied my face with ore dust and then laid down by the ship's side and let the boys pile dunnage wood over me and my haversack which still contained a couple of Canadian biscuits and a bottle of water. They were careful to do it in such a manner that, if detected, I could assert with confidence that I had stowed away without contact with, or assistance from, the crew. It was not a really comfortable berth. Before long the bangs of beam handling and the clatter of hatch boards ceased. There was a short period of near silence after the last dockers had departed. Then there was music indeed in my ears. Clang, clang, clang, went the engine-room telegraph, 'Stand-by Engines.' Soon it rang again, 'Slow ahead,' it must have said, for the diesel engines responded with hiss, chuff-bomp-bomp-bomp as they started, and sent a shudder of life through the whole ship. What heavenly sounds! How marvellous to feel the ship under way! When we were clear of the docks and the pilot had rung 'Full ahead', the boys had a chance to slip down into the 'tween deck and dis-inter the uncomfortable stowaway.

They took me to one of the crew's cabins, a room for two which was an innovation in the days of crews' fo'c's'les. This was inhabited by Motorman Ivar Persson and Motorman Stig Fågelberg, who made me warmly welcome. It appeared that this cabin had been chosen because its location was handy for unobtrusive entry into the 'tween deck, and on account of the character of its two occupants. Erik clearly wished to limit the number of people who knew of the existence of the unauthorized passenger, particularly whilst there was a German pilot aboard.

The journey down the Elbe passed without incident. In the evening the rhythmic beat of the engine slowed, then stopped. The anchor cable rattled out of the hawse pipe. Full astern on the engine. Stop. LUOSSA was anchored in the mouth of the river off Brunsbüttel for the night.

The crew were on watches but Erik and his pals came in and there was an animated exchange of yarns.. They brought me more food, excellent Swedish fare, which I ate with great relish. And a real bed, with clean white sheets, was made up for me on the deck in the space under one of the bunks. It was long since I had enjoyed such luxury. Though I still had to run the gauntlet of the Gestapo next day, I had by now learnt the lesson about taking 'no heed for the morrow', and, thankful for one of the most adventurous days in my life, I fell into a dreamless sleep.

The Gestapo's Net

Early next morning the German canal pilot came aboard and LUOSSA hove up anchor and entered the Kiel Canal at the Brunsbüttel lock. Nisse Larsson, the crew's mess boy, brought me a sumptuous breakfast – well, I reflected, if the damned Gestapo did catch me I would at least start with a good full belly. The black-out shutters on the cabin port holes in the ship's side were kept shut during manoeuvres into and out of the lock. But, when the ship was under way in the 53-mile long canal, Ivar opened them. I spent the time pleasantly enough looking out and watching *der Vaterland* slide past.

Eventually, Erik, Edvin and another A.B., Charles Blücher, came to the cabin and, as planned, took me with all my escape gear into the 'tween deck. As before, I dirtied myself up a bit and then the boys buried me under a big pile of dunnage wood. I wasn't too uncomfortable lying on the deck by the ship's side and felt I could stand it for a few hours without making noisy movements that might betray my presence. The engine-room telegraph rang. The engine stopped. This must be Kiel. There was a faint sound of shouting between the sailors and the rope handlers ashore in the lock. A pilot ladder rattled down the ship's side and soon there was the ominous sound of steel-shod jackboots tramping on the deck. I heard my heart beating too. This was the danger point. It all depended on the thoroughness with which the Gestapo conducted the search. Erik and co. had tried to assure me that LUOSSA had passed through the canal so many times without incident that, as a rule, the Gestapo didn't spend much time aboard. But I was well aware of how thorough they could be, particularly if they had been tipped off about my escape, or if by chance there had been a break-out from another Camp, or if a zealous Nazi in command might do it just for the hell of it and to show the neutrals who the *Herrenvolk* were. The tramping of jack-boots and accompanying noises, seemed to go on interminably. Lying there it was hard to tell whether the noise came from the main deck overhead or from men in the 'tween deck and it was hard to keep account of time. I wished my watch had a luminous dial. Suddenly the noises stopped. Silence reigned awhile. The telegraph clanged. The diesel engine went bomp-bomp-bomp again. The ship shook as the propeller threshed the water and pushed her into the Baltic sea; at least, that's what I imagined. Soon they stopped again. Had she been stopped to drop the pilot of for some other reason? In the cramped darkness of my hide-out all sorts of imaginary reasons raced through my mind. Perhaps the real search was only just about to be started. Then – clang, clang, clang, bomp-bomp-bomp-bomp. Half ahead. Clang, clang, clang again – that was full ahead. The good old LUOSSA shook as the engine drove her up to maximum speed. Was it true? Freedom at last?

LUOSSA docked at Oxelösund that Saturday evening, 28th August. The scheme was that I should go through the dock gate with a few others, posing as a member of the crew. An identification document had to be shown, so one of the boys, whose photograph resembled my features, lent me his Seaman's Book. His name, appropriately enough, was Stig Friman.

When all were ready, faces shining with soap, muscular bodies evident under shore-going suits, we trooped down the gangway on to the quay. Swedish soil at last! Friendly Sweden! Near the gate a dock policeman sat in an office which had a window like a railway ticket office. Each man in turn put his book on the shelf for examination and, as he did so, spoke though the aperture saying the ship's name, LUOSSA. He looked at my book and myself no more thoroughly than the others, which was just as well for Stig's personal particulars showed him to be head and shoulders taller than me. Outside the dock gate the party split up. One returned aboard with the borrowed book, the rest arranged to rendezvous later.

Great-hearted Erik took me to his lodging at the home of Mr. and Mrs. Carlsson in Oxelösund. They, dear people, took me in without hesitation.

Before long, Erik and I went by train the ten miles or so to Nyköping, where we met our shipmates at a first class restaurant. A table had been booked. After an appetizer at the bar, we sat down at the meal-table which was bedecked with luxurious white, starched napery and beautiful table-ware. The smörgåsbord was an amazing sight. I could help myself to whatever I fancied. This was the first time for over two years that I had had a real choice of menu. Smoked salmon would be perfectly satisfactory as an hors-d'oeuvre, I thought. Swedish sailors ashore could be just as punctilious in their table manners and etiquette as their landsmen. I was glad I knew their customs, particularly regarding 'skåling', so that I didn't unwittingly cause offence. As the meal progressed, accompanied by brännvin and wine, the atmosphere became even more relaxed and tongues more ready to talk. Erik stood up and, with dignity seldom matched outside Scandinavia, formally welcomed me to Sweden. I could not have wished for a better opportunity than this to express my heartfelt thanks to these gallant men who, at risk to themselves, and without promise of reward, had brought me out of Germany and treated me in this handsome fashion. I could only hope my Swedish was good enough to convey to them my profound gratitude for what they had done for me.

This party in itself would have seemed a fitting climax to my safe arrival in Sweden, but there was more to come. We all went to the local cinema and saw Noel Coward's **'In Which We Serve'**, the film about war service in the Royal Navy, a story of quiet heroism completely free of bombast or crude propaganda. It filled me with pride and gave me hope that civilized values still existed in Britain, even after four years of warfare.

Chapter Seventeen

Stockholm Interlude

A fast electric train whisked me off to the capital on the Monday morning. Stockholm, a wonderful city in a beautiful setting, is a good place to be at any time, but it was heaven for me on that bright autumn day.

I made straight for the British Legation (it was not an embassy at this date) to report my arrival in Sweden and to give an account of myself to the Naval and Military Attachés.

When the preliminary reporting was completed, my kindly interlocutors turned their attention to my personal welfare. 'Have you any money?' 'I have a few kronor which the good fellows of LUOSSA gave me. I guess I can subsist for a couple of days. What about getting home?' I was informed that an air link was maintained with Britain, but wait for a passage was inevitable and the date of departure quite unpredictable. 'Well, have you got a job for me to do in the meanwhile? Something contributing to the war effort, for preference?' They thought it likely that some help in the Chancery would be welcome, and undertook to make enquiries. 'You'll need a lodging, of course,' the Military Attaché remarked. 'I'll see if one of my officers could take you in.' 'What about my clothes? I have only the ones I am wearing, I borrowed them from the sailors and promised to return them as soon as possible.' They remembered then that I was in the Merchant Navy, and said they would put me in touch with the Consul General whose job it was to look after non-services personnel. So off I trotted to the Consulate where arrangements were made to rig me out. With this fairy godmother act initiated, other matters important to the official mind, to which I confess I had paid scant regard, were broached. 'I suppose you didn't bring your passport with you,' the Consul General said, with a twinkle in his eye. Taking my cue from him, I proffered my forged German 'ausweis'. Of more concern than the lack of a passport, which could be put right soon enough , was my admission that I had not reported my arrival to the Swedish authorities. In short, I was an illegal immigrant.

The Consul arranged for me to see the Swedish police. I arrived punctually for the appointment, only to be told that the English-speaking officer had just gone to lunch. Would it be convenient for Herr Bird to return in an hour and a half's time? With so much more to get done before the Legation closed, I reckoned the unexpected delay would be quite inconvenient. With a smile, I said in my best Swedish, 'If you would excuse me for misusing your language, for which I have a great affection and respect, I dare say I could answer your questions in Swedish.' The officer was obviously pleased that an Englishman should have troubled to learn his language, and he immediately agreed to try my suggestion. By pretending that I did not understand I was able to avoid direct replies to some of the questions I did not wish to answer. I was able to conceal the fact that I had had any assistance from the crew of the ship on which I admitted I had stowed away. 'What was the name of the ship?' 'Really, I have no idea, it was night time when I stowed away and it was dark when I crept ashore and got into a goods wagon in the dock sidings which brought me to Stockholm; so I couldn't even say which port I landed at.' 'So you really landed without anybody seeing you?' I smiled and said, 'When one had managed to evade all the armed guards hemming one in, in the Third Reich, it is not so difficult to make a quiet entry into dear old friendly Sweden.' Luckily he accepted this bit of bluff, and after making a few more notes he bade me a friendly farewell.

I was glad I had avoided making any remark that might have betrayed the involvement of my stout friends of LUOSSA in my escape. My anxiety would have been even greater if I had known at the interview that the officer whose patriotism I had flattered was a Nazi sympathizer and in touch with the Germans.

Back in the Legation, I was offered the job of Bag Messenger as soon as security clearance had been obtained from the Foreign Office. I realized then that they hadn't taken my story at its face value.

It was a relief to hear that my parents would be informed of my safe arrival in Sweden, through the Foreign Office. And, now, with a stay in Stockholm in prospect, exciting possibilities sprang to mind –

if only I could get a similar message through to Norway. Tentative enquiry into this revealed that not only could it be done but that it would be done secretly, forthwith.

Just before the office closed, I was introduced to Mr. E. J. Wright, who had kindly agreed to put me up, and we walked together to his home where I received a warm welcome. Almost at once it seemed worth spending a couple of years in prison to have the privilege of living in this unique household. The head of the family, known as 'Pop' to us all, was a splendid product of the regular army, a towering presence, yet kind and quite unflappable. Dear Alice, his wife, was vivacious, good looking and loquacious in the nicest possible manner. She was a wonderful mother to all who came under that hospitable roof – and a superb cook. John was the youngest child, a schoolboy full of promise. Mary, still at college was a gay spark with a good dash of innocent mischief about her, but she also had a lot going on behind her sparkling eyes. Dinkie, just twenty-one, was the most beautiful young lady that any man could dream of meeting. Her charm was not merely superficial, for she was intelligent, an accomplished pianist, practical and jolly good fun to know. As she walked to the Legation through the park, with her Afghan hound 'Nicodemus', this glorious vision of feminine elegance turned everybody's head. And here was I, entrusted with the same door key!

There was yet one more permanent resident, Harry Battley, a nice big man, worldly-wise, ex-Scotland Yard, and now in charge of security at the Legation. I enjoyed his company and was to be involved in several 'Holmesian' adventures with him in due course.

From time to time Bangergatan 10 took in other waifs inside its friendly portals. It was always an open house to any of the British community who chose to pop in. On Sundays, Alice, Yorkshire to the core, treated all and sundry to her speciality – 'Yorkshire Pudding'.

Being a Bag Messenger turned out to be a more interesting job than its name suggested. It included conveyance in safe custody of the diplomatic mail bags between Bromma Airport and the Legation, and, of course, in the reverse direction. This was always done during the hours of darkness, for in pre-radar days it was safer to fly across the North Sea at night.

It was great fun for me to sit in the airport lounge with Germans chatting away in the next seats while I waited for our aircraft to arrive.

Dakotas and Mosquitos were the machines used on this service. Unarmed they were flown by B.O.A.C.[1] pilots. When I went on to the tarmac to collect the bags, I never knew who would come out of the bomb bay of a 'mossie' when the door swung open. It might be a new junior clerk, or Malcolm Sargent arriving to conduct the Stockholm Philharmonic Orchestra.

The flight to Scotland was not without danger of attack from the Luftwaffe; in fact, some planes were shot down. I attended one that had made a forced landing beside Lake Vänern. This provided me with the rare experience of chartering a private train, at least a locomotive and one wagon, to get the bags and airmen safely to Stockholm.

Fortune smiled again, after my personal particulars had arrived on the desk of the Chief Security Officer at the Foreign Office in London. By amazing coincidence my father had worked for his father many years before, so he knew me from childhood. This resulted in a doubling of the salary I had been offered and, what was even more satisfying, I was invited to work in the Chancery in the daytime. Among my various interesting tasks in the 'holy of holies' was reading typed despatches and comparing them with their authors' manuscripts. These gave glimpses of the truth behind the news, which was often quite revealing; and the telling phraseology the Secretaries sometimes used, was the obverse of that commonly thought of as 'diplomatic'.

An event that gave me great satisfaction at this time was the procurement of a shore job for my gallant helper Erik Solberg of m.v. LUOSSA by Mr. Mitcheson, the Commercial Attaché. Through his business connections he was able to get him placed in a Unilever factory, and so Erik got out of the iron ore trade with Germany that he detested and he was soon able to get married.

---

[1]*British Overseas Airways Corporation, predecessors of British Airways.*

CHAPTER EIGHTEEN

Edel's Story

Far away in the middle of Norway, a handsome young man strode up to a farmhouse door and knocked. Farmer Kristian Thomassen and his wife Nelly had seen the stranger coming and noticed that he had left his car a hundred yards or so down the road. They were suspicious for few people other than Germans drove motor cars in those days. The farmer opened the door, not knowing what to expect, and was surprised when the young man introduced himself as a friend of his daughter, Edel, and asked if he might speak to her. There was an air about the young fellow that disarmed suspicion, so he was told that Edel was with her sister in the nearby town of Hamar. If his business was important, he could meet her there. He said that he would like to see her; thereupon Thomassen gave him the address and said goodbye. Still puzzling as to what it was all about, he telephoned Hamar to say the stranger was coming.

Edel and her sister, Hjördis, waited in keen anticipation. The stranger was admitted at once and Hjördis, sensing something unusual, left them alone. In quiet tones he announced that he was a member of the resistance movement and that he had a message for her. From a secret pocket he produced a folded slip of paper and handed it to her. The five words on it went through her like an electric current. In a haze of emotion she heard the young man say, 'You had better come with me to Oslo now.' Edel was not of the swooning kind, or the message and the peremptory request to leave home that instant with a complete stranger would have bowled her over. She asked if she could have an hour or two to prepare. The young man was adamant. 'No, I must go to Oslo at once and I can't say how you could otherwise get there.' He insisted that she should tell no-one what was afoot. Edel quickly explained that her brother Kristian was also active in the 'underground' and had a car and illegal petrol, so there would be no difficulty about that part of the journey. That settled it. She gave him the address at which she would stay in Oslo. They shook hands and he departed.

What an overwhelming change could come about in less than five minutes! Now, like a conspirator, she had to deal with the family and somehow wriggle round the truth. Her parents were told that her doctor had recommended that she should see a specialist in Oslo about an ailment they knew had been troubling her for some time. A telephone call to the Karlsons secured her accommodation in town. To lie to her folk and continue to deceive them was an ordeal, and she feared there might be worse to come if things went wrong.

Four days later, her brother Kristian drove her the eighty kilometres to Oslo. She had left her food ration book at home, to avert suspicion, and took a little food with her to tide her over the odd day she expected to be with her friends, the Karlson family. Much to her embarrassment, several days passed and still she received no orders to move. There were mysterious telephone calls for her every day, apparently intended to reassure her that all was well; but they didn't allay her anxiety over eating the Karlson's starvation rations. Several complete strangers called to speak to her, and one of them looked a very rough type indeed. Luckily, she had been able to suggest that any personal visitors should call at the tradesmen's entrance and ring E (dot) T (dash) on the bell to warn her to answer the door. She had made up her mind to tell the Karlsons the truth about her visit when a man called and said, 'Be on platform 3 at the East Station tomorrow morning at seven o'clock. I will take your suitcase now; you just carry your toilet things with you.' It was with difficulty that she acted normally for the rest of the day.

At seven o'clock precisely on Thursday, 14th October, 1943, Edel took up her position on platform 3 as instructed. A man approached. She recognized the unprepossessing figure who had previously called at Karlsons. Without obviously engaging her in conversation, he managed to tell her that a young lady would come and take charge of her. After a furtive glance around, he surreptitiously passed an envelope to her and said, 'Here are 100 Swedish kronor and a false passport. Memorize your name and particulars when it's safe to do so.' With that he sidled off.

There were few people about and none near, so she stole a look at her passport. She saw that she was a seamstress.

Shortly, a beautiful, very well dressed, young lady approached and, as if they were old friends, said, 'I have the ticket, we'll take the next train to Mysen.' Edel enquired about her luggage. 'Don't worry about that; you are in the hands of a first-class travel agent!'

At their destination they went into a little cafe, and with no more than a nod and smile from the girl, the proprietor served ersatz coffee and sandwiches. It was rather a strain engaging in small talk, for hours on end, under the pretence that they were well acquainted. Suddenly the girl said, 'I must go out, you sit here, I won't be long.'

Presently she returned and said, 'It's all right. We'll go in a few minutes. No explanation was given and Edel was wise enough to act as if this was all part of her normal routine of life. They boarded a country bus that drove off immediately and bumped along the by-ways, stopping at isolated farms en route to drop a parcel here or pick up a passenger there. After a long drive, it drew up at a farm and the girl stood up, indicating without a word that they should alight. The pair went to the farm worker's cottage and were admitted without ceremony. The man and his wife and their five-year-old child showed no sign of surprise that a complete stranger was with the lady they knew. While they were eating a light meal the little girl began asking embarrassing questions; 'What is your name auntie? Where have you come from?' As it wasn't yet the child's bedtime, it was suggested that Edel should rest in another room, after the meal, to relieve the situation. 'You have a strenuous night before you, you had better rest,' the woman whispered as she closed the bedroom door. Sleep for Edel was out of the question with all the unusual events of the day whirling around in her mind. At least she could rest her body.

At 10.00 p.m. she was called and got up. The smart young lady had disappeared and, to Edel's surprise, the rough fellow had taken her place. 'We'll be off in a few minutes,' he said. 'Can you ride a bike?' Edel nodded. Two machines were produced and the pair set off. It was a beautiful, moonlit night, clear and crisp, with about 5°C of frost. The spiky tops of the pine trees were silhouetted against the starry sky. After a while, it might have been any time from a half to one hour's riding, the man stopped. They dismounted and he said,

'We'll leave your bike here.' He took the machine and hid it among the trees. 'Now I'll have to carry you on my bike. Can you get on the crossbar?' Edel suggested that the carrier might be more comfortable, and sat on it. On they went, he now labouring with the extra load, along the undulating road, she gripping her little attaché case and keeping balance as best she could. There was no sound save the creaking of the overloaded carrier and the occasional 'thwack' as a tyre shot a small stone into the roadside bushes. 'A car's coming,' Edel warned. The beams of headlamps waved up and down as the vehicle in the far distance bumped along the rough road. 'Germans! Jump off and hide,' he said and then rode away, leaving her on the roadside in a fairly open tract of farmland. Edel saw the dark shape of a barn a hundred yards away and ran towards it. She got into the shadow of the inclined bridge up to the loft, and as the lamps played on it crept round in the moving shadow till the big staff car had passed. She stood there, still panting from her exertions, feeling alone, very much alone, and a bit upset by the incident.

In a short time the guide returned and said they must proceed on foot. They walked in silence and entered a very dense and dark pine forest. Eventually Edel whispered, 'I can hear voices.' they stood still and listened. 'That's O.K.,' he said, and they walked towards the sound. Suddenly they came to a clearing beside a lake where a small group of people stood talking in low tones, audible only because of the stillness of the night. They walked up to the party. There was no greeting or word of introduction, but among the group was the attractive girl again. A boat was at the lakeside, with an oarsman at the ready. The girl asked the company to get into the boat and she followed them, but the rough man disappeared without saying a word. The boatman dipped his oars so gently, and pulled on them so carefully, that their progress was almost noiseless. At the far side, with a whispered caution for silence, the boatman and the girl led the party up the bank and on to a metalled road. After a quarter of a mile or so, they passed a couple of farmhouses all blacked-out and asleep, and just beyond them was a cottage, which they entered. Edel could now take stock of her companions. There was a woman with a child in arms, another who was pregnant, a lame Frenchman called André and a couple of other men, as well as the boatman and the occupants of the cottage.

There was something else in that room that most of them had not seen in the last three years – slices of beautiful white bread and butter and loads of cheese. They were invited to eat, and fell on that sumptuous fare like hungry wolves.

Some time past midnight (it was now 15th October), the order was given to prepare to depart. Ominously, the pretty girl examined an automatic pistol with the air of expert familiarity, before placing it in a holster strapped round her slim waist. She and the boatman led the group along a narrow path, through the thick forest over rough ground, which was hard going for the two women, who obviously were 'townies', and especially for the lame Frenchman. Quite suddenly, the profound silence of the night was rent by screams from the child. The noise must have been audible for miles around. Visions of 'Who goes there?', arrest and being thrown into the dreaded Grini concentration camp flashed through their minds. But the pretty girl was not dismayed. As if by instinctive reflex, she produced and administered a drug that put the little child to sleep within seconds. Progress was not as fast as the guides wished, but they were very solicitous of the pace-setting Frenchman, for the poor fellow had got his injuries at the hands of the Nazis. In the tense atmosphere that the conditions generated, the journey seemed long. After stumbling along for a few miles through the forest, they abruptly stepped out into a wide clearing that stretched away on either side as far as the eye could see in the bright moonlight. Somebody whispered the thrilling words, 'The Frontier'. Freedom was just over there. They were excited but apprehensive. The boatman and the girl were reassuringly calm. 'We two will leave you now,' the girl said. 'There are no guards hereabouts tonight. Give us your passes.' As if to reinforce their optimistic remark, they lit a small fire of pine twigs and carefully burnt the forged documents. With the fragrant aroma of pinewood smoke wafting around them, the pretty girl laconically announced, 'You have just got to walk across this clearing and you will be in Sweden. 'Good bye, and good luck!'

As they made their way across the clearing, there was a sense almost of anti-climax. Not a challenge. Not a shot. There was no doubting the efficiency of the courageous men and women in the underground network of the 'Home Front'. Once on the other side of that invisible divide, Edel felt as if a great load had been lifted from her shoulders. She guessed the others felt the same, for there were broad smiles and congratulatory handshakes all round.

Proceeding as previously instructed, the party eventually spotted lights that led them to a Swedish Military outpost. They were challenged by the sentry, who immediately called out the guard. It was quickly established that the strangers were refugees and had no hostile intent. So the soldiers received them in a very friendly fashion, inviting them into one of the two huts on the site. It had a single open room with bunks around the walls, tables and bench seats in the middle, and a stove was alight casting welcoming beams of warmth on to the newcomers. A great plate of white bread, thickly buttered, was soon put on the table and was quickly devoured. It was almost with embarrassment that the refugees accepted a third plateful of that lovely food, and in between mouthfuls drank hot coffee of a quality not tasted for years.

Weary as she was after this day of continual excitement and emotional stress, Edel could do no more than doze fitfully as she lay fully dressed on one of the bunks. So it came as a relief when a soldier called them at seven o'clock and brought coffee, bread and butter. Good hot coffee!

Soon an army lorry arrived for them. The mother and her child and the mother-to-be were put in the driver's big cab. Edel, wrapped in a military great coat, went in the back with the rest of the party. They were driven to a temporary medical centre that had been set up in a village hall. Evidently they were not the first refugees to take this route. A doctor and nurse checked to make sure they were in good health. Formalities completed they were driven to a guest house where they were fed and housed overnight. What a joy to see and mix, unafraid, with free, uninhibited and friendly Swedes. It seemed unreal. No Germans, no Quislings and no fear.

The next day saw Edel and her companions on a train, which was clean and bright, not soiled by war traffic and neglect as were the trains of Norway.

The farmhouses en route were nicely painted, just as Norwegian farms had been in happier times. The train stopped for some minutes at Karlstad, where kindly Swedish folk, evidently expecting them, served coffee and cakes, a gesture that was much appreciated. The destination was a refugee clearing centre run by the Norwegian Government-in-exile. 'Kjesäter' had been the large country house of a wealthy private person. Now its accommodation had been supplemented by several wooden barracks erected in the grounds. Some were offices. One was used as a dormitory, another as a dining hall. Obviously 'Kjesäter' housed a sizeable community, and it served as the filter of the stream of refugees who, for one reason or another, had had to escape from Norway. they included Home Front workers fleeing for their lives, and other patriots hoping to join the Norwegian forces. There were wives of previous escapers and some unhappy women, pregnant by German soldiers, who dared not face the music at home. All had crossed the border somewhere, somehow.

Edel was soon launched on a tour of the twenty or so offices for interrogation. Personal particulars were naturally the first to be registered. 'Ah, you are Miss Edel Thomassen? I have a note here that your suitcase is in the store room in Hut No. 3. Perhaps you would like to collect it during the day?' So the pretty girl's quip about the first class travel agency was after all not just a joke. The questioning on her war-time activities in Norway, an extremely vigorous examination for some, as she learned later, was relatively light. Perhaps this was because they seemed to know already all about her brother Kristian's work and the family's staunch anti-Quisling stance. Nevertheless the inquisition was not completed that day. The next, being Sunday, was a day of rest, so the de-briefing spilled over into Monday. 'What can you tell us about German activities in and around Hamar?' 'Is it true that they requisitioned such and such a farmhouse three weeks ago? 'We have some evidence that Mr. 'X' is a Quisling. If so, it may be significant to us that he's keeping very quiet about it. Have you any positive knowledge of him in this connection?'

Tuesday, 19th October, 1943, dawned, a fine autumn day full of promise. Conscious that Fate was at work, Edel boarded the train for Stockholm. Her pulse quickened as the train rushed along through forest and farmland. Her thoughts raced: 'Four years and four months have passed since we made our vows and were parted. What will he look like now? Will he have changed?' The three golden crowns on Stockholm's beautiful Town Hall glistened in the sunshine as the train slowed down through the suburbs. Nearer and nearer came the magic moment. Edel was leaning out of the window. She saw me waving. As the train came to a standstill she jumped out and ran towards me.

Is It A Dream?

Edel and I immediately began making arrangements for our so long delayed wedding. Who knew how many day's grace we had before we should be parted again? Conscious of the hand of Providence that had so wonderfully re-united us, we were intent on having a religious ceremony. It would have to be a very quiet affair, for, among other reasons, we had hardly any money. The Reverend Clement Jones, Chaplain of the British Community, would publish the banns in a Swedish church which his congregation shared in the winter months because of the shortage of fuel oil for heating. So our unpretentious plans were made for the service to take place there on Saturday, 20th November, 1943. Luckily, Edel had smuggled out of Norway a few hundred kronor and was able to exchange enough of them to buy herself a wedding ring.

How naive we were! Dear Alice and Pop, backed up by the whole British Colony, and a few Scandinavians too, had quite different ideas. Sensing the romance of the occasion, they took matters into their own hands and elevated our humble nuptials into the realm of fairy stories.

The ladies decided that the bride must be suitably attired for the role they were creating for her, and they carried it through in fine style. Mrs. Mallet the Minister's wife, laid the foundations by giving her elegant underwear. A Swedish lady lent a Paris model wedding gown and long white kid gloves. Other warm-hearted ladies made sure that none of the essential etceteras was wanting. And, lest the day should be cold, Mrs. Labouchere, the wife of the Second

Secretary, lent her a splendid mink coat.

The bridegroom's wardrobe also needed attention. My one-and-only suit was scarcely in keeping with the Paris bridal gown. Happily, one of the Secretaries came to the rescue with an introduction to his tailor – and mercifully, that carried a bit of credit!

Fuel shortages notwithstanding, the ceremony would now take place in the picturesque and typically Anglican church standing in its park-like setting of trees and lawns.

The great-hearted Wright family determined to hold a reception for us at No. 10, and sent out the invitations. Marvellous presents of a practical nature poured in from many well-wishers, and very many more chose to express their sentiments by generously contributing cash to a fund sponsored by the indefatigable Military Attaché, Colonel Sutton-Pratt, who presented us with a sum of money that quite took our breath away. This heart-warming stream of spontaneous sympathy and generosity stirred us deeply.

In spite of this general euphoria, our feet were of necessity kept firmly on the ground. Edel continued to go out doing housework (which was permitted) to bring in a few kronor. And as if to remind us that a bloody war was still raging and claiming urgent attention, there were regrets of absence from, among others, Captain Henry Denham, R.N., the Naval Attaché (with a big bank note enclosed!). As for myself, on the great day there was no risk of staying abed too long with a stag party hang-over, for I had to go to Bromma to meet a plane at five o'clock in the morning.

Inside the church, early afternoon, it was not only comfortably warm, but to my surprise and delight, it was tastefully decorated with flowers – expensive at that season – through the kindness of Mrs. Helmi Jones and helpers.

Accustomed as I had become to experiencing the marvellous, I could scarcely believe it was myself standing at the chancel steps in front of a large congregation, waiting for my bride, my best man, Lieutenant Dan Gibson-Harris, R.N., Naval Attaché, at my side.

On cue, the organist struck up, 'Here comes the bride', and Edel came up the aisle on Pop's arm. Nor was my sense of unreality lessened when I saw her radiant in an elegant white silk gown and carrying a bouquet of roses.

The Rev. Clement Jones performed the ceremony with great feeling and gave an address which caught the exciting romantic atmosphere that everyone felt. Then as man and wife we started on our journey into the future – walking slowly between rows of well-wishers, some in tears, to the majestic strains of Mendelssohn's Wedding March.

The response to the invitations to the reception stretched the ample accommodation of No. 10 to the limit. We were privileged to have the company of about fifty guests who ranged in social status – as commonly reckoned – from Mr. Mallett[1], the Minister himself, to my fellow Bag Messenger.

Alice, her family and other helpers, excelled themselves with the catering despite the prevalent food rationing. Otto Johansen, an expatriate Norwegian baker, had made the wedding cake. And after the traditional cutting of it by the bride and groom, toasts were drunk in champagne donated by Colonel Sutton-Pratt.

An interesting feature of this great cocoon of affection that had been spun around us was the fact that neither of us had known any of these dear people before we arrived in Sweden, except for two Norwegians and two Swedes.

We were proud to have three escapers among our guests, namely, Lieutenant Michael Codner, Flight Lieutenant Oliver Philpots and Flight Lieutenant Eric Williams, who had recently won their freedom through their amazing escape through the Wooden Horse.

Suitable speeches were made and telegrams read, including one from my parents and sister, who were, perforce, rejoicing at thome in England. The only cloud on our horizon at that moment was the thought that Edel's parents had no idea what had become of her.

Our joy was to continue, for our generous friends had even arranged a short honeymoon for us at the luxurious Grand Hotel at Saltsjöbaden; a beautiful and romantic spot in the archipelago, not far from Stockholm.

One night, early in the New Year, we boarded a Dakota and ran the Nazi gauntlet for six hours on the way to Britain. We were received joyfully into my family. Edel joined the Land Army, as a

---

[1] *Subsequently Sir Victor Mallett.*

farmer's daughter should; and I went back to sea in m.v. ARMADALE. It was an uncanny experience to tread the decks of this identical twin of the dear old AUSTRALIND.

Dick and Edel Bird's Wedding Photograph, Stockholm, 20th November, 1943

Appendix 1

The German Rations

Daily
Bread	318.0 gm.	=	11.200 oz.
Jam or Syrup	25.0 gm.	=	0.875 oz.
Margarine	21.0 gm.	=	0.753 oz.
Sugar	25.0 gm.	=	0.875 oz.
Tea ('mint')	1.4 gm.	=	0.050 oz.
Coffee (ersatz)	1.5 gm.	=	0.050 oz.
Meat (including skin and bone)	35.7 gm.	=	1.250 oz.
Fat	9.7 gm.	=	0.250 oz.
Potatoes (including skin and waste)	525.0 gm.	=	18.450 oz.

Every Other Day
Vegetables (mostly sauerkraut and swedes)	500.0 gm.	=	17.500 oz.

Items on 9 Day Ration
Noodles	50.0 gm.	=	1.750 oz.
Oats	50.0 gm.	=	1.750 oz.
Semolina	50.0 gm.	=	1.750 oz.
Barley	50.0 gm.	=	1.750 oz.
Salt Gherkins	150.0 gm.	=	5.250 oz.

Twice a Month
Cheese	31.25 gm.	=	1.090 oz.

Substitutes might be given for any of the items listed above.

Everything on the list that needed cooking was simply boiled in great coppers and made into a characterless soup. The sauerkraut and swedes were cooked and doled out separately and so were some of the potatoes at a later date.

The author is indebted to Mr. W. Errington, Cadet ex-S.S. DEVON for this list which he copied on 16.11.1944, while working in the camp office. It is not known how closely the rations received tallied with this list. It is doubtful if our five thin slices of black bread weighed anywhere near 11 oz., dense as it was. Certainly the potatoes must have shrunk a lot in the cooking!

Appendix 2

The following is a list of typical contents of the standard food parcels sent by the British Red Cross Society.

    1 Tin biscuits, such as Service Ration, Krispbread, etc.
    1 Tin cheese
    1 Packet chocolate
    1 Tin fish, such as herrings, pilchards, sardines, etc.
    1 Packet dried fruit, such as dates, prunes, raisins, etc.
or 1 Tin pudding, such as apple, treacle, creamed rice, etc.
    1 Tin honey or jam or marmalade or syrup
    1 Tin margarine
    1 Tin cold meat, such as ham and beef roll, galantine, pressed beef, etc.
    1 Tin hot meat, such as curried mutton, minced steak, steak and kidney pudding, etc.
    1 Tin milk
    1 Tablet soap, unscented
    1 Tin sugar
    1 Packet tea
    1 Tin vegetables, such as beans, peas, spinach, etc.
    1 Tin special food with Ascorbic Acid (containing Vitamin C), such as fruit bars, lemon curd, etc.

and one or more of the following:
    Cocoa, Ovaltine, etc.
    Ginger nuts, etc.
    Marmite, Yeastex, etc.
    Meat or fish paste
    Oatmeal
    Condiments
    Sweets, such as barley sugar, butterscotch, etc., and other articles as available.

Tobacco and cigarettes were packed separately every week.

Appendix 3

As distinct from the British Red Cross Parcels, the contents of the Canadian parcels were standard, i.e. always the same in kind, quantity and quality.

1 lb. tin of butter
1 lb. tin of powdered milk 'KLIM'
4 oz. tin of tea or coffee
12 oz. tin of corned beef
8 oz. tin of meat roll
1 oz. tin of sardines
1 oz. tin of salmon
1 pkt. of biscuits
4 oz. packet of cheese
8 oz. tin of jam
5 oz. bar of chocolate
4 oz. pkt of sugar
1 pkt. of raisins
1 pkt. of prunes
1 pkt. of pepper and salt
1 tablet of soap
50 cigarettes

Appendix 4

Extracts from the Log of Cadet William Errington, ex-S.S. DEVON.

1945
March 5th
Today is the big day. We are all getting our parcels today. Later – we all got 100 cigarettes – Yanks; but they certainly taste good after Polish, French and Yugoslav. It's a lovely feeling to be back to normal.

March 7th
All feeling the benefit of better feeding, although 'spuds' are hard to get these days. The German ration is about two per day. Terrific raid over Bremen and Westermunde tonight.

March 8th
The greatest news yet! Our troops have crossed the Rhine. Now we can expect the fireworks to start. Another big raid tonight. Started on Camp Wood gang today.

March 15th
Capt. Aldridge and Dr. Campbell have left camp to attend some sort of conference in Berlin. We wonder what for. Major Harvey refused to go.

March 16th
Major Harvey left under protest at four o'clock this morning to attend conference. Rations cut again today.

March 17th
Terrific rumours are going round. The Germans are going to bump us all off. We are a hindrance to the war effort. They have already started on the Russians and Poles. Aren't we lucky!

March 18th
Doctors returned from Berlin and brought disturbing news.
1) There is a severe outbreak of typhus sweeping the country. 2) German rations are liable to cease altogether in the near future. 3) We cannot expect any help from the Germans as they can hardly make ends meet for themselves. We are all to receive inoculations against typhus. We are warned to keep clear of any refugees. We must conserve all food possible as we most probably shan't get any more after a week or two. We in this camp are very lucky, other camps are in an appalling state, many dying of hunger and some committing suicide. Many camps have typhus already. Things are becoming chaotic. But what can we do? Just wait hopelessly.

March 20th
Definitely known that Himmler made a speech the other day. In it he said: 'The Germans may fall under pressure but if the people must take chances the allied prisoners shall also take those same chances.' In other words they mean to keep us till the last if possible. So we may expect to shift soon. What a life!!

March 22nd
Still working in the wood gang although several jobs have stopped lately. Germans seem to be confining as many as possible to the Camp.

March 24th
Montgomery's forces have crossed the Rhine at Wesel. You cannot imagine the excitement in the camp at present. Everyone is very optimistic. They are only 140 miles away now and they say their objective is Hamburg and Bremen. It's impossible to think that we may be home in a month or so.

March 30th
Rumours are coming in fast and furious now. But they are so wild that it is hard to believe them. There have been some terrific raids lately.

April 2nd

Now definite they have captured Munster. In which case they are about 100 miles away. I wonder if the Weser will hold them up. I'm praying that it won't. We get strafing planes over every day now and the raids are becoming more frequent.

April 4th

I don't think the Weser will stop our troops now. News says that we have reached Weser at Minden; in which case they are about sixty miles away. Everyone in the Camp is completely off balance. Some say the war for us will be over next week. I hope so but I don't believe it.

April 6th

They are coming still nearer. The Weser was crossed last night. The strain in the Camp will be terrific soon. Everyone keeps thinking they can hear the guns.

April 7th

It hardly seems possible. Twenty miles from Bremen and they say there is no opposition. The foremost fear in everyone's mind is that we might be shifted east of the Elbe, but I hope not. I don't think many of us would make it. The R.A.F. are strafing all roads continually, day and night.

April 8th

Today's latest. Twelve kilometres from Bremen. It doesn't bear thinking of. So near and yet so far (we are only about fifteen miles from Bremen). We may be free in a few days' time.

April 9th

What a hell of a time we've had today. First thing this morning the Germans closed the gates and no one at all was allowed out of the Camp. Of course that started rumours flying round. Then at three o'clock we had a 'muster' for all hands and the Navy (Marlag M) were told to be ready packed to leave Camp at five o'clock. That means 600-700 were to go on the march. (Also Ilag and Marlag were leaving across the way.) Chaos ensued while the Navy prepared for the march. At five o'clock there was no sign of them being ready.

Then at 5.20 word came over that the Navy and Airforce Officers had refused to leave. So things have been left over till tomorrow.

Now for the best news of all. The Germans are beating it from here as fast as they can. They started moving about six o'clock tonight. For the last three or four hours farm carts have been queuing up at the 'Provien' Barrack outside the gate, collecting all the stores and carting them away. The *'Posterns'* are all packing and preparing for flight. The Germans informed Capt. Notman that they were leaving the district and were taking the R.A.F. and Navy prisoners with them. Civilians and Merchant Navy were being left behind and were to be guarded by a skeleton crew of guards and officers who were to hand the camp over to the British when they came.

Then the Camp started to go mad. First, prisoners tore down the warning wire and got rid of the matting which cut off our view of the outside world. As it got dark people came out with wire cutters and forced their way out through the barbed wire. Some went to the Provien Barrack and stole cases of alcohol and at this moment there are wild bottle parties going on all over the place. The guard towers were invaded and the searchlights and telephones stolen for souvenirs. Then they began breaking up all fencing and towers for firewood. Through all this turmoil the German guards are standing helplessly by, watching and unable to do anything as they have no definite orders about us. Artillery has been heard all day long in the direction of Bremen and planes have been flying round the vicinity strafing all day long. If these blokes do have to march there will be quite a few mown down by our own planes, worse luck. As it gets dark we are able to see a bright red glow in the sky in the direction of Verden on the Weser which is about twenty miles away, and they are strafing the Bremen-Hamburg autobahn which runs about four miles south of the Camp.

There are quite a few hundred people outside the camp tonight. Earlier on, the Germans brought the thirty-six paratroopers (just captured and being interrogated in Dulag) to the gate. They are supposed to be marching with the others. They had been standing around talking to our chaps behind the wires, receiving cigarettes, food, etc. One or two of us managed to get outside during the turmoil and mix with them. We suggested they should take off their berets and badges and walk back in as prisoners. Wonder of wonders!! The plan succeeded and about five or six managed to get in. Capt. Notman in the meanwhile was trying to get them into the camp so that they could have a good meal before they left. At about 8.30 they were all sent in to us and Capt. Notman advised them to scatter and hide. There are rumours that the Navy aren't going to leave, they intend to hide if possible. We shall see tomorrow probably. It's going to be difficult hiding 600-700 men.

April 10th
The fireworks started at daylight. The village was strafed at dawn this morning. So we were all out of our bunks early. At ten o'clock the Germans ordered a muster for all hands, for the purpose of collecting the Navy together. As a result the whole Navy went into hiding up at our end of the camp. We had six hiding in our room alone, so I suppose other rooms must have been the same. The Germans came in with machine guns, Tommy guns, rifles and hand grenades and they really looked like business. They started searching from the bottom of the camp and worked up to our end. They were firing up into the rafters and below the barracks to bring anyone out who was unlucky enough to be there. In all they collected about 150. They were put on the road and marched off at 3.00 p.m. We mustered later again and we were told that the deadline was 4.00 p.m., i.e. they were collecting as many as possible up till then and then evacuating. While we were on appel the T.A.F. came over and started strafing the road by Ostertimke. Immediately we thought of that column. We now wonder if it really was our chaps they were shooting up. The 'Underground Navy' as we call them should be pretty safe now. The number in our room has gone up to eighteen now. They are sleeping in cupboards and on tables and benches, but I don't think it will be for long.

April 11th
As we thought it was our column they were strafing yesterday. Five were killed and six wounded. I wonder how many will reach their

destination? We had more appels today but there are only about 100 odd Germans left now so the searching was not very thorough. Already we hear that most of the column has escaped and are hiding in the woods round here. They'll probably wait a few days and then come back to the camp when all is clear.

April 12th
Some of the Navy and R.A.F. chaps are beginning to drift in now. The T.A.F. has been over in force today strafing the roads and villages. Tanks and heavy lorries have been passing through all day today, heading East.

April 13th
Nothing unusual. The news is very contradictory and you cannot rely on it. People are still drifting in from the woods. Order came out today: No-one to leave camp except on official business. Anyone disobeying orders will be handed over to Military Authorities when they arrive.

April 16th
Nothing but rumours and T.A.F. Rumour says that we are surrounded. It seems like it because at intervals we can see and hear artillery fire all round us. It can't be long now.

April 17th
Had my worst scare today. Was working in the wood yard outside the camp. The yard is about 100 yards from the road. The T.A.F. came over and spotted some lorries on the road at the crossroads. There is a belt of trees between the yard and the road. The planes were over the trees and firing before we even knew they were there. The bullets were going over us, but did we scatter!! It gave me a funny feeling to know they were our own planes.

April 19th
We awoke to the same old things. Troops no nearer yet, but they still seem to be all round us. Then at about 6.00 p.m. the rumours started. Our troops made a rapid advance and reached Zevern which is only

seven miles away. At 8.30 there was a muster for everyone on the Main *Platz* and Capt. Wilson made a speech. The troops were definitely only six or seven miles away. The Germans were evacuating and leaving about forty or fifty men under command of Korvetten Kapitan Rogge who was to hand us over to the British. Marines and Navy were paraded and told that we were taking over control of the camp. So tomorrow we shall wake to see our own men parading the wire. Wilson expects us to be liberated (what a word!) tomorrow. We won't get much sleep now.

April 20th
The final assault on Bremen started about 6.00 p.m. tonight. They are simply raining shells into the town. It's just one continual rumble and the camp is vibrating the whole time. We are definitely surrounded now. Our forces are advancing from south, east and north. The guns are getting nearer all the time. The camp was bombed and strafed last night. Six killed and six wounded.

April 22nd
We can see the R.A.F.. bombing Zevern. If they come much nearer I think the barracks will give way. Prisoners are coming in who say they were only caught about four miles away.

April 25th
Zevern has fallen and the troops are advancing west towards us. Our water and light supply has been cut off completely.

April 26th
The fun and games started at 10.00 a.m. this morning. Our troops started shelling Ostertimke and Kirktimke. The latter is on a hill about 1½ miles away. The German artillery is replying from Kirktimke and Bulstead. In other words there is an artillery barrage going on and we are in 'No man's land'. While I am writing this, shells are bursting all over the place. The nearest we've had yet is ¼ mile away.

This afternoon at one o'clock Captain Rogge left for the British Lines. He went to negotiate for an armistice while we are evacuated from here to the British. Capt. Notman has ordered the camp to be ready to march any time after 3.00 p.m. So at last I shall find use for my home-made haversack. Pandemonium reigns in the room. Clothes, books and food are being thrown out left and right.

At 5.00 p.m. we heard officially that Capt. Rogge had passed through the British Lines with Lieutenant Henkin and an A.D.C. of the General's. We don't know when he is expected back, but the whole camp is ready to move at a minute's notice. The firing is still going on.

10.00 p.m. Still no news. We are turning in, all standing, tonight. The firing has died down somewhat.

April 27th
Comparatively quiet last night. There is still no word of Rogge. The A.D.C. returned to the German lines last night but the other two are still behind the British lines. Going out on the wood gang this morning but there's not much work to do.

11.00 a.m. While working on the wood the Germans have brought some *'Nebel-werfers'* into the field. They are firing them from Bilstead right over the camp to Kirktimke. They make the most horrible whining whistling noise I've heard.

2.00 p.m. The Germans are bringing guns and tanks, etc., into Westertimke. In other words about 100 yards from our Barrack. We are right close to the wire here and the nearest farm is about forty yards away. They are bringing up guns and digging themselves in. We in the north end of the camp have been advised to evacuate down south end. The hospital is already moved into the Theatre. The Top Galley has ceased to function. While I'm writing troops are going into action down the Bilstead road, carrying *Panzer-Fausts* and machine guns, etc. People all over the camp are frantically digging themselves trenches and dugouts. I think things are going to be really hectic soon. There is a solid wall of smoke sweeping towards us from Kirktimke direction. It is raining steadily and visibility is about ½ mile. In fact a real 'No-man's land' atmosphere. Our trenches are about two feet deep with water. I wish Rogge would come back and give us a definite answer whether we are to go or stay. It's such a horrible feeling to be behind barbed wire and having no arms or ammunition and no protection. Machine gun fire is growing more frequent from the south-east and it's getting nearer I think. We in the room are debating whether to evacuate or stay here and funnily enough we have a gramophone going full blast. They are playing 'Some day soon' at the moment. Very appropriate. What!

The people who have my sympathy at the moment are the children in the village. They are coming in from the outlying districts. As they come down the road shells start to whine overhead and a child of five or six does a 'belly flop' straight into the ditches at the side of the road. It's funny how the slightest shelter seems to give you comfort.

The gun at the farm at the corner here has started, firing into Kirktimke. If the British locate this gun I'm afraid we are in for a hot time. I think we shall definitely evacuate now. I mean to say forty yards off the mark is good shooting for artillery when they are doing blind firing.

I thought so. This is being written in the trenches. All hell has been let loose (5.00 p.m.). Shell fire on both sides. I'm almost too excited to write. They say Germans from Bremen are heading this way to reinforce the area. British pressing hard from Kirktimke probably to relieve us. They've mined the village, ready for evacuation. Just going out for a look round.

From where we are we can see the road. Just now Germans are pulling out hell bound, with shells bursting all round them.

Other tanks have started up from Bremen and have pulled into some trees about fifty yards away, probably a delaying action so that others can get out.

Things have quietened down a bit now, only small arms fire but plenty of it. Our troops are in the village. Maxie and Stoker (experts) can recognise our guns. They must be only fifty yards away, some of 'em.

Once it used to be 'only a few years now', then 'only a few months', then 'only a few weeks and days'. Now it looks very like a 'few minutes' before FREEDOM.

Time 7.20 Vickers firing just over other side of barrack (at least it sounds like it). Germans pulling out again.

7.30. German infantry pulling out now. Under continuous shell fire. Shells landing thirty to fifty yards from camp wire. Germans keeping close to wire whilst retreating. Last self-propelled gun is pulling out now under continuous fire. Planes overhead now. First time today. British seem to have lifted range of guns, going over camp now, landing west of village. Germans gone through woods west of the camp. For the first time for an hour or so there has been deathly quiet for two minutes. Started again. No, only one rifle shot. Here comes another whine – over she goes – quiet again. We expect village to go up any minute.

7.45. We're nipping out now to make cocoa. And still the birds sing in the trees. Everything still quiet but a couple of Germans are still in the house across the road. Probably snipers.

8.20. Opened up again. Albert said just now. In middle of action old German of sixty odd was walking round wire picking up dumpers. Most of prisoners are in bottom of camp (about 3,000) but I think it's safer here somehow.

9.00. Self-propelled gun which was west of the outskirts of the village just fired five or six rounds and is now pulling out along Tormstads road. We think it is the last – no, another one has just started up. Shrapnel has been raining down all over the place for some time now. It's dark enough now to see tracers from our bullets. They are obviously in our village.

9.30. It is all small arms fire now with just an occasional burst of shell fire. There are periods of dead quiet broken by short bursts and the tinkling of glass.

Just now we could hear our own troops shouting to one another. There was one chap whistling as he went along then he'd give a burst of fire and carry on whistling. They seem to be mopping up the troops in the farms.

9.40. Terrific fire has started near Lager 3. I think it's some of the barracks on fire. All quiet now and we are thinking of trying to snatch a few hours sleep.

10.50. Small arms fire started in village again. You should have seen our sleeping quarters. Most of room 9 have evacuated so we commandeered the room. Jack and Maxie slept under a bunk which had been pulled up under concrete of chimney. Mac slept on top of the bunk. I started off by lying under Dai's bunk but couldn't manoeuvre so I evacuated to Hick's bunk.

11.47. I was dozing off to sleep when Stoker shot up in his bunk and said, 'What's that? Did you hear anyone shout.' They said, 'Hello there, is that a P.O.W. camp?'

I was out of my bunk like a shot and straight out of the window. We ran like hell over to the wire. What a terrific sensation. A couple of blokes were standing just by the tower, both had on tin helmets. It was a beautiful sight. I was too full for words. After all these years I could only stand and gape at them. One of them, a Sergeant, said, in a strong Scots accent. 'Hello there. Is this Milag Prison Camp?'. Somebody managed to gibber a reply. Then an officer came up and told one of the men to cut a way through the wire. He asked us how we were getting on and if everyone was safe. Lieutenant Hart was there and he gave him all the dope about us. The Tank Officer asked if there was anything we needed in the camp and the only thing we really needed was water. That, he said, was impossible. They hadn't got any.

In the meantime the Sergeant had cut his way through to us and the first thing we did was to shake hands with the first free British man we had seen for four years. He gave us his hip flask and I had my first drink of rum. I often wanted to taste it, but I am glad I didn't, because it was very appropriate that it should be the first drink I should have in freedom.

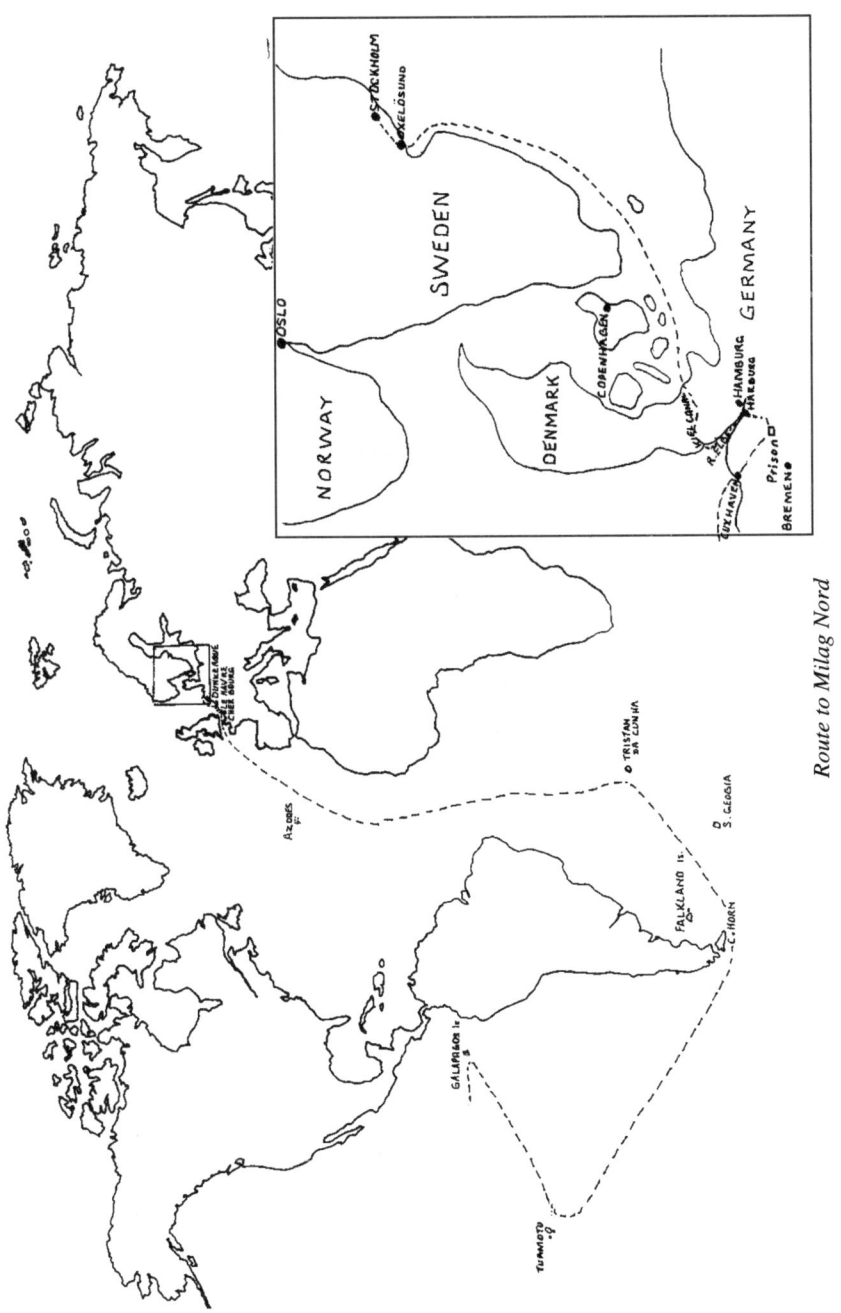

Route to Milag Nord

195

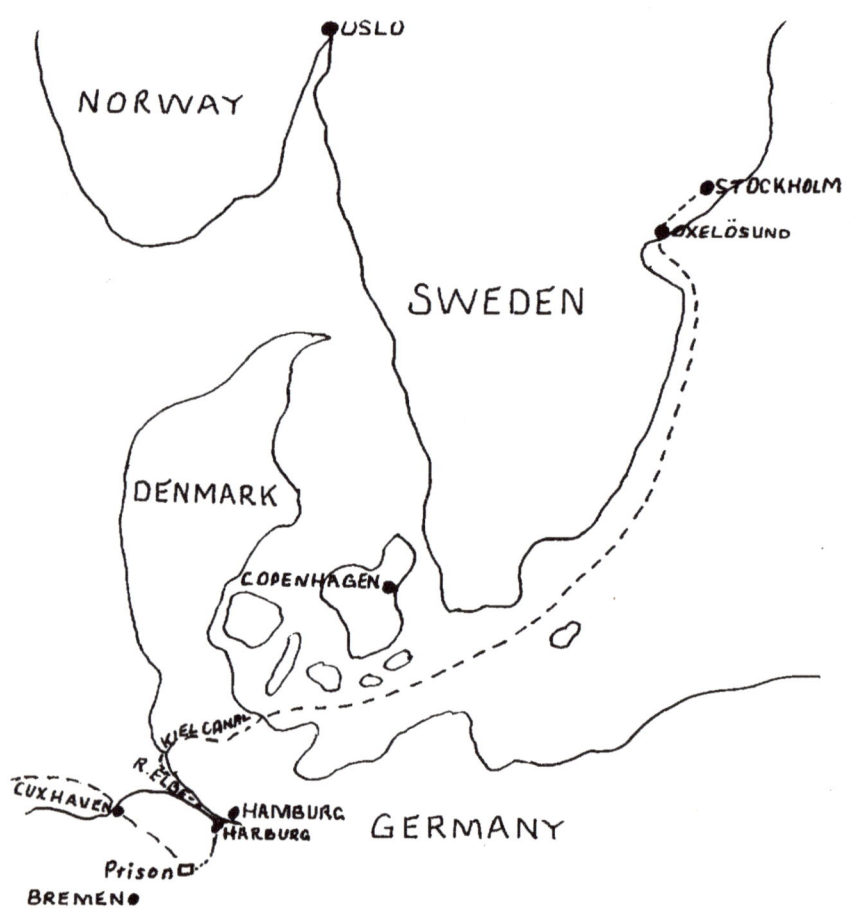

Escape route from Milag Nord to Sweden